THE EASTENDERS
PROGRAMME GUIDE

THE EASTENDERS
PROGRAMME GUIDE

Josephine Monroe

First published in 1994 by
Virgin Books
an imprint of Virgin Publishing Ltd
332 Ladbroke Grove
London
W10 5AH

Text copyright © Josephine Monroe, 1994
EastEnders copyright © BBC Television Ltd 1994

Typeset by CentraCet Ltd, Cambridge
Printed and bound by Cox & Wyman Ltd, Reading,
Berks

ISBN 0 863 69825 5

CONTENTS

For Vicky Mayer

Many people have helped me write this book and I would like to thank Siân Pattenden, Joanne Higgs, Richard Arnold, Nikki Groocock and Sara Bache and Fenella Mantle in the *EastEnders* publicity office for all their help (and for putting up with me).

INTRODUCTION

Right from the very first episode, *EastEnders* was a phenomenal success, and it quickly became a national institution. Audiences hovered around 20 million, soaring to an astounding 30 million for one episode, as half the country became gripped by the humorous, dramatic and tragic events in Albert Square.

Tourists started asking London cabbies to take them to Walford, and bookies started taking bets on who the father of Michelle's baby was. *EastEnders* had arrived – and British TV would never be the same again.

The success of this soap was in its realism. Never before had a TV show depicted daily life with so many warts, split ends and hangovers! The set was so believable that it had people looking up Albert Square, Walford, London E20 on the map. The litter, the weeds and half-derelict buildings were a first. Previous soaps had created a place where viewers would want to live. But no one in their right mind would choose to live somewhere so grotty and where the only ray of sunshine falls off the back of a lorry. But people wanted to watch *EastEnders* because they *believed* it, and they cared about the characters.

Suddenly, everyone knew a Dot Cotton and every local publican was likened to Dennis Watts. For the first time people watched a show and said, 'That could be me.'

The two people responsible for Albert Square and its residents are the show's creators Julia Smith and Tony Holland. Julia and Tony already had quite a reputation within the industry, having made their names on shows such as *Angels* and *District Nurse*. They were originally approached by the BBC to develop a twice-a-week 'soap' in March 1983, and the BBC asked them to consider two proposals they had already received about a shopping arcade and a caravan park.

But Tony wanted to create a show about something he knew about, something he could make people believe in. And he didn't have to look far for his inspiration. His mum Ethel came from a big East End family where several generations lived under one roof. Tony knew how they would stick together in public but fight and cry behind closed doors, and he knew it would make unmissable drama. So he and Julia decided that their soap would centre around just such a family.

They wanted to set the soap in a classic Victorian square and started regular visits to London's East End to do some serious research. But the East End they found wasn't exactly what they remembered from their childhoods. Traditional fruit and veg markets had stalls selling Indian spices and fresh Jamaican patties, and many of the pubs had been turned into wine bars. The yuppies, they observed, had arrived and were exerting yet another new influence on the area.

The East End had become a melting pot for modern society, although it was still deeply entrenched in its past. Evidence remained of the Blitz bombings, but more importantly, it was still home to families like Tony's.

The duo worked hard on their project persuading the BBC to buy the old ATV studios at Elstree as a site for the new show. Tony and Julia were constantly bombarded by phone calls and meetings, and because of crossed wires in the communications channels, ended up with only 40 minutes to write and type their original proposal for the BBC bosses.

They were at BBC TV centre in Shepherds Bush, hoping to have a chat about market research, when a secretary informed them of their imminent deadline. They grabbed pen and paper and rushed across the road to the Albertine wine bar. It was 6.20 p.m. on 1 February 1984, and they had until their meeting at 7 p.m. to outline the most important show in the BBC's history. But they did it, and the bosses loved it.

All they had to do now was invent some characters! So they took themselves away for two weeks to somewhere where there was no phone and no interruptions – Lanzarote. Tony and Julia sat in separate rooms in their rented apartment, and divided the responsibilities between them. Tony would take care of the main family, and Julia would create the rest.

Many of the Beales and the Fowlers come straight out of Tony's family album. His aunt Lou had married an Albert Beale – and Tony even has cousins called Pete and Pauline! This traditional dynasty was an important inclusion in the cast as they helped convey the East End maxim: blood is thicker than water.

Tony's real-life family also provided much of the drama for the on-screen Beales. It was his memories of large Christmas dinners and family conferences that gave Pete, Pauline and their clan their breath of life. The Beales also give *EastEnders* a sense of history – they belong in Albert Square and they'll fight for their home tooth and nail.

An important element of the original line-up was the high number of single characters, people who lived alone like so many modern Londoners. First there was Ethel, based on a spritely old dame the duo had spotted in a pub. Other misfits were Lofty, punk mum Mary and Dr Legg, a reserved old man who knew more about the locals than he would ever tell. His affection for Albert Square later became clear when he revealed that his bride of only two months had been killed by the bomb which demolished the house behind the Queen Victoria Pub in 1940. (The replacement at number 47 is a typical 1960s-built maisonette.)

Many of the names for these characters came straight from tombstones in East End graveyards. The brewery which owns the Vic, Luxford and Copley, was named in such a way. The name for the Square itself was simple: they had always been talking about a Victorian square, so Queen Victoria's husband Prince Albert was the obvious inspiration. The monarch herself was reserved for the pub. Bridge Street was the only choice for the road off the

Square, given the rusty railway bridge that dominates it. Turpin Road's namesake was that legendary local highwayman – a reminder of the East End's criminal connections.

Julia and Tony thought that yuppies wouldn't have quite made it to Walford yet, but Debs (a bank clerk) and Andy (a nurse) at number 43 would try to fill that role.

The immigrants they had seen during their recces to the real East End would be depicted by Tony and Kelvin Carpenter, a West Indian builder and his academic son; Bangladeshis Saeed and Naima Jeffrey, partners in an arranged and sexless marriage who run the local convenience store; and Ali Osman, a Turkish Cypriot married to English wife Sue, who owns the local café.

The characters they had difficulty creating were the tempestuous creatures who inhabited the Vic. Julia devised Jack, Pearl and Tracey Watts, but as the characters began to come to life they decided on their own names – Den, Angie and Sharon. And the rest, as they say down Bridge Street market, is history.

But once they had decided that the murder of Reg Cox would be the show's first major storyline, Tony and Julia realised that none of their new friends were capable of such a deed. So they begat Nick 'Rotten' Cotton, a local boy turned sour who had pure evil in his blood.

The next task was to devise the storylines for the months to come, and as Tony knew his characters so well, they came easily. He knew that Michelle would soon be pregnant (and he knew who the father was); he knew that Den and Angie would split up; and he had an inkling that one day – in the distant future – their daughter Sharon would return triumphantly to the pub that was once her home.

In the immediate future though, he had to find a name for the new soap. It had had the working title East 8, but that sounded like 'Estate' when spoken quickly. 'E8', 'Round The Square', 'Round The Houses', and 'London Pride' were put forward before they realised they had been using the title everyday, in practically every sentence – *EastEnders*.

Keith Harris was roped in to design the Square (and all the interior sets) and he insisted on building the set ahead of schedule so it could be allowed to 'weather' before filming began. Keith's attention to detail meant walls had to be torn down because they were too straight! He wanted the bricks to be crooked and have moss growing on them.

Although the new soap wasn't due to air until early 1985, Tony started assembling a writing team in May 1984. The early scripts would be crucial and to make sure they were just right he commissioned different writers to write episodes one and two. His hunch proved a success; the competition between the two writers (Jane Hollowood and Gerry Huxham) inspired both of them to produce truly remarkable dialogue. In the end, Tony and Julia decided Gerry's version of episode one was ever so slightly more suitable than Jane's, but Jane's episode two was better than Gerry's.

The next hurdle was casting. Some characters found their alter ego easily. Bill Treacher fitted Arthur Fowler's clothes so easily it was as if he was meant for the role. In fact the Beales and the Fowlers came together pretty swiftly, and they looked alike and behaved like a family when they were together. Julia had decided that she didn't want anyone 'famous' in the cast so as not to distract the viewers from the characters, but Wendy Richard (well known from *Are You Being Served?* and *The Newcomers*) persuaded Julia she wanted to play a woman her own age, and was cast as frumpy Pauline Fowler. Susan Tully was a familiar face from *Grange Hill* (she played rebel Suzanne Ross) but she bowled the duo over as Michelle and was offered the part.

Leslie Grantham thought he'd audition for the part of Pete but was offered villainous Den instead. But casting his wife Angie was problematical. No one quite seemed right, but a talented actress called Jean Fennell won the part as she'd convinced everyone she'd grow into Angie. But when Julia Smith saw her first scenes on film, she felt in her bones that Jean just wasn't quite right. She couldn't put her finger on it, but Julia knew she would have to go through with the painful task of letting Jean go.

And that caused a major problem. They were already three days into filming and Julia had no idea who could replace her. But then she remembered an actress she had once taught drama to – Anita Dobson.

Anita read for the role at lunchtime, and by the end of the afternoon had been fitted for costumes and handed a pile of scripts. She was perfect. Her energy ignited the whole cast and gave *EastEnders* the confidence it needed.

The first episode aired at 7 p.m. on 19 February 1985, and 17 million viewers tuned in to hear Den utter the show's first words: 'Stinks in here.' The instant success made *EastEnders* legitimate fodder for the tabloids, and three days later the front page of the *Sun* had the headline: 'EASTENDERS STAR IS KILLER'. Somehow they had found out about Leslie Grantham's conviction for manslaughter while he was in the army in Germany. And so began a love-hate relationship with the Press.

The papers became so interested in Leslie that it required more security to sneak him into the studio than Princess Diana needed on her visit! But the coverage in the media guaranteed huge viewing figures, which reached a staggering 30 million for the episode on Christmas Day 1986 when Den handed Angie the divorce papers. At the time it was the highest-ever British TV audience on record.

EastEnders has continued to confound the critics and delight its fans. Its attention to detail (the flashy knock-off clothes, the plastic daffodils 'planted' six weeks before season so when the episode airs nothing looks out of place, and Vicki's jumper that reads 'Walford Primary School') means nothing jars when you watch it. For an hour every week, you can truly believe that Albert Square is a real place, and that the tears and triumphs of its residents are all real too. You can even smell the bacon frying in the café. And it's pure heaven.

THE EASTENDERS

THE BEALES AND THE FOWLERS

A member of the Beale family has lived at 45 Albert Square since well before World War II, and there'll probably be one there forever. The family is as much a part of the East End as jellied eels and pie and mash.

The Beales and the Fowlers provide the backbone of *EastEnders* – their traditional values remain constant when everything else in their lives changes.

The men in the family tend to be a bit weak, henpecked by their strong wives and invincible mothers. Theirs is a matriarchal society with Lou Beale uncrowned queen.

Lou came into her own during the war when her beloved husband Albert went off to fight for his country, leaving Lou to take care of the house, and their three kids, Kenny and twins Pete and Pauline.

Lou thrived on being in control – she was her own boss and she loved it. So when Albert died she was quick to take control and make sure things were just how she wanted them. And woe betide anyone who sought to change them!

Lou loved interfering, specially in her children's lives. She vetted prospective partners and always disapproved, and nothing anyone could say would ever alter her opinion.

But she could also show great compassion. When granddaughter Michelle got pregnant it was Lou she confided in because she knew that Lou would give her a fair hearing, and offer sound advice. But if she thought you'd done wrong, Lou wouldn't spare your feelings. 'Well, if the truth hurts . . .' she'd say, and it usually did. Whether you were family or not, you lived in fear of the old battleaxe.

In 1963, her favourite son Pete came home and announced he was getting married. Lou's heart sank – he was only eighteen and she had always hoped for more from Pete. Pete had always wanted more for himself too, he had dreams of playing in a band or becoming a Butlins Redcoat.

But his girlfriend Pat Harris – the local tart – was pregnant and he had been brought up to do the right thing, so even Lou had to grudgingly give her consent to the marriage.

After the shotgun wedding, it turned out the pregnancy was a false alarm and Pete was trapped in a charade of a marriage to a woman he didn't love. However, they soon had their own child, David.

He found comfort with a pretty local teenager, Kathy, and when she agreed to marry him he left Pat, even though Pat was again pregnant. Kathy may have been young, but she had grown up in the slum area of Walford with tough brothers and an alcoholic father, and so she came to the family with her own murky and painful past.

Lou was surprisingly calm about Pete walking out on his first wife – but that was because she knew that Pete wasn't the unborn child's father. Lou suspected that this was Kenny.

Disgusted with Kenny for sleeping with his brother's wife, Lou made him pack his bags. Kenny emigrated to New Zealand where he married and had a daughter, Elizabeth.

Pat never understood why Lou had kept her secret, but she was always grateful. The truth was that Lou didn't want Pete hurt. Anyway, he and Kathy were well on their way to producing their own son, Ian.

Many years later, Pat returned to the Square and confessed that neither Pete nor Kenny was Simon's father. The boy's real father was Brian Wicks – a man with whom she had been having an affair and later married. But from the way she told it, it was clear she really couldn't be sure which man was the father.

Pauline, meanwhile, had met Arthur Fowler, a local

lad with little panache but a heart of gold. One day Pauline was due to be bridesmaid at a friend's wedding but she had a severe bout of flu and had to pull out. Considerate Arthur came round to make her feel a bit better and found himself proposing to her to cheer her up.

As she was about to give her answer, she noticed that his collar was turned in. And as she straightened it, she realised that here was a kind, good man who needed taking care of. So she said yes.

(Many years later when their daughter Michelle was dithering over marrying another sweet, kind local lad, Michelle asked her mum why she'd married her dad, and Pauline told her about the collar. Michelle realised she was marrying Lofty for the wrong reasons and resolved to call the wedding off. But the next time she saw Lofty, his collar, too, was all tucked inside itself. So just like her mother, Michelle also married a man she would have to take care of – all because the hapless men couldn't tie their ties properly!)

Pauline and Arthur never set the world on fire, but they were good to each other and over the years came to love each other very deeply, although they rarely expressed those feelings. They suited each other down to the ground – they even had the same taste in drab cardigans – but neither of them was very good at being romantic or taking the initiative, and the spark eventually disappeared from their relationship.

The Fowlers had three children: Mark, a moody rebel who always flirted with the law; Michelle, a year younger than her brother but always mature beyond her years and who carried on the family tradition of strong women; and little Martin, an unexpected added extra who arrived when Pauline was 43.

Arthur was often out of work and the couple could never quite afford to move out of Lou's house. And Lou never tired of telling Arthur how he failed as a provider, and consequently he never felt like that house was his home until Lou died in 1988. As if he wasn't undermined enough by his circumstances, Lou always put the boot in where Arthur was concerned. Lou's constant bickering whittled away at Arthur's self-confidence, and as a consequence Pauline became stronger to compensate.

In the end Pauline made herself so indispensable to daily life in Walford that everyone leant on her. Eventually this role got to her – she even ran away for a night just to prove her point – but if the truth be told, Pauline quite enjoys listening to other people's woes. After all, they're a good source of gossip.

And the gossip is usually about 'family'. The Beales and the Fowlers are never far from the centre of action in *EastEnders*. Pete will always be part of any lynch mob out for natural East End justice, and as the local fruit and veg man he always had a direct line to all the Square chitchat. Michelle will often be the centre of the crisis, and Mark, quiet and reserved, will be going through hell in silence.

The family has endured many a trauma. Shortly after Pauline's own pregnancy, sixteen-year-old Michelle became pregnant – and refused to name the father. She later married Lofty in the registry office – but not before she'd jilted him at the altar. Mark ran away because he was in trouble with the law (and Nick Cotton); Arthur had a breakdown and ended up in jail after stealing the money to pay for Michelle's wedding.

Pete's 'son' Simon sped into the Square in October 1985 driving a flash yellow Spitfire and dragging up the past. The sharp-dressed lad with his blow-dried hair and wing-tip collars was a first for Walford, and his presence ruffled a few feathers – notably those of his little 'brother' Ian, who felt forgotten when Wicksy arrived.

Kathy's past returned to haunt her when she was blackmailed by local villain Nick Cotton. He had stolen her medical records and discovered she'd been raped as a teenager. Suddenly capable Kath was seen to be weak, but – survivor that she is – she pulled through only to have fate deal her a cruel double blow when she was raped again in 1988 by local toff, James Willmott-Brown.

The propensity for drama was obviously genetic as Ian found himself in an almost identical situation to his father.

Ian married market-stall worker Cindy Williams, believing that the child she was carrying was his. In fact, it was his 'brother' Simon's. Belatedly, Simon (Wicksy) decided to assume his paternal duties, and Cindy and baby Steven ran away with him, leaving Ian distraught and bitter.

This bitterness meant Ian worked harder than before – anything to take his mind off his pain – and he built up a successful catering business, the Meal Machine. His anger also made him ruthless and he is now a major force to be reckoned with round the Square. Ian has finally become the man his father always wanted him to be (Pete was always worried his son was a 'poof' because Ian had wanted to be a chef). And when Ian decided he wanted Cindy back, it was on his own terms.

Pete always took the macho thing too far. He joined the local 'Westerners Society' (don't dare call it a Cowboys Club) and took to wearing a ten-gallon hat because he dreamed of being as heroic as John Wayne. Everyone told him he looked stupid in the hat, and eventually he swapped it for his famous tweed number.

Pete was so desperate to prove himself to his dead father (he would often spend hours sitting on Albert's grave asking for advice and approval), that he had a tendency to demand things of his family.

Pauline would jump whenever he asked (even though he was only five minutes older than her, she always looked up to him), but Kathy and Ian needed a gentler touch. His blunt manner was no support when Kathy was raped, and in the end she left him because he couldn't, or wouldn't, understand what she was going through.

After many lonely years as a single man, and after comical attempts at finding love through a video-dating agency, Pete finally met Rose Chapman, a girl he'd gone to school with.

There was an instant attraction, and they wanted to be

together at any cost. But there was a snag – Rose was the wife of renowned local villain, Alfie Chapman.

So one night they disappeared, never to be heard of again until December 1993 when two policemen came knocking on Pauline's door and announced they had bad news. Pete and Rose had taken a chance on returning home, but on the way, their car had been involved in a crash and they had both been killed. Pete's death was made even more poignant by the arrival of his twin grandchildren by Ian on the same day.

Pauline and Arthur trundled along as usual, unaware that their marriage was becoming a habit. Their joy at Mark's return to Walford turned to fear and worry when he revealed he was HIV positive, adding yet another strain to their marriage.

Mark's ex-girlfriend Gill Robinson arrived in Albert Square in 1992. Like most of Mark's lovers she was an older woman and she too had the HIV virus. When this developed into AIDS, Mark took care of her and ended up falling deeply in love with her. He married her only to watch her die the next day, knowing that one day, maybe soon, his family would watch him die too.

When Pauline went to New Zealand to care for Kenny after a heart attack, Arthur – who was now running a small gardening business – started working for Mrs Hewitt, a bored suburban housewife who developed quite a soft spot for him.

Arthur resisted her offers until Pauline returned home and her pompous attitude ('Walford's horrible and drab, New Zealand's marvellous') drove him straight into Christine Hewitt's arms.

Eventually he confessed his affair to Pauline who was so stunned and angry that she hit him over the head with a frying pan! Ineffectual as ever, Arthur could not make Pauline forgive or understand him, so he ran away and stayed in a dosshouse until he was spotted by Frank and brought back to the Square by Michelle. On his return, he was able to move back into number 45 to care for Martin while Pauline was on holiday.

She was adamant that he could not be forgiven for his betrayal, and the family has never been the same since. The affair is rarely mentioned these days, but it has left a painful and unsightly scar on the whole family.

DEN AND ANGIE

Against the grey and gritty background of Albert Square, local publicans Den and Angie Watts stood out like glorious cocktails in a sea of cheap beer.

They were the Square's centrepiece: feisty, cunning and passionate. Him in his flash suits and her in her flashier jumpers, they trail-blazed through life in Albert Square. But they were an unholy alliance and they tore each other apart. Dr Legg summed up their relationship when he commented over his pint: 'Tragic. I've never seen two people more suited to each other.'

And it was tragic. They had been childhood sweethearts and married when Angie was just eighteen. He was the good-looking leader of the pack, and she was the sassy and pretty Cockney sparrow.

But it all turned sour. After just a few years of marriage, Den lost his appeal for Angie and they started to sleep in separate beds. Maybe it was this early sexual rejection that made him Walford's most notorious womaniser. Most couples would have split in these circumstances, but Den and Angie needed each other and they stayed together. Besides, they had the Queen Vic to run and their differences were never allowed to upset the punters.

Both Angie and Den had grown up in Walford, and as they saw their great mates Pete and Kathy, and Pauline and Arthur, work at their marriages, the Wattses decided that they would fight to stay together too.

They adopted Sharon in the hope that she could re-kindle their passion, and for a time it worked. But Angie started drinking and Den started seeing other women, and from then on it was war!

Angie's addiction to gin was surpassed only by her addiction to Den – she was hopelessly devoted to the rotter. And although he was now in love with Jan, an upmarket executive, he was flattered by her devotion and couldn't bear to leave Angie – or the Vic.

The pub became their battleground and poor little Sharon was their ammunition. In fact it seemed they loved each other (and loved fighting each other) so ferociously that they often forgot they had a daughter. Scoring points off the other was more fun, and possibly more important.

Den tried to make it up to his little princess by buying her things, but all Sharon wanted was to be loved and given some guidance. Consequently she grew up to be a teenager starved of affection and came close to going off the rails.

Not that Angie and Den weren't proud of Sharon. Angie was practically moved to tears when Sharon sang at the Vic one night. Every bone in her body willed Sharon to be the success that she truly believed she would be.

The Wattses were perfect publicans. Angie kept two sets of books, just so Den could flog booze that had fallen off the back of a lorry owned by one of his underworld associates. Angie, with her East End charm, would entice the drinkers to get drunk, and Den, with his own brand of charm, would throw them out when they fell over.

In 1985, when Angie discovered Den had gone on holiday to Spain with his mistress, their spats became childish. Any opportunity to rub the other's nose in any failings was seized upon. Angie started to flirt openly with the customers, while Den stole every minute he could to talk on the phone to Jan. She had brief affairs with neighbours Tony Carpenter and Andy O'Brien, and he, impulsively, spent the night with Sharon's best friend Michelle.

Things came to a head for Den and Angie in February 1986 when, in the middle of a crowded evening session,

Jan walked into the Vic looking for Den's support as her father had just died.

Jan had entered not only Angie's territory, but her castle – the one place that truly mattered to her – and that could not be ignored. It was time for a showdown!

Den was torn between comforting Jan and pacifying Angie, and in the end did both. He told Angie he was leaving both of them and moving to a bedsit. Naturally, it was a lie – he had really moved in with Jan.

When Angie discovered his deceit and realised that Jan (or Miss Silk Knickers as she used to call her) had won the prize, she took an overdose. She borrowed some of Dot's prescription pills, and begged for pills and potions from most of the women in the Square. But no one guessed what she was planning. And one night in March she stuffed a handful of the assorted pills into her mouth like sweeties, and washed them down with a swig of gin.

Coincidentally, Den had argued with Jan and returned to the Vic in the early hours to find Angie, comatose, slumped over the kitchen table. He picked her up and walked her round, pleading, 'Don't die, Angie, don't die.' He called an ambulance which arrived just in time to pump her stomach and save her life. After a couple of days in hospital, Angie returned to the Queen Victoria to find Den extra-attentive (and slightly guilty) and planning a recuperative holiday in Ibiza. Jan, he promised, was out of the picture.

Yet again they tried to make a go of their marriage, and yet again they failed, and eventually Den told Angie he wanted a divorce. To hold on to Den now would require every ounce of Walford cunning that Angie had – she would have to pull something spectacular out of the bag to keep him this time.

Convincingly, and with great vulnerability she told her husband that she only had six months to live. She had a liver complaint, 'All that drinking you see.'

Unwilling to disbelieve her in case it was true, Den said he would stick by her and make her last months mean

18

something. But he promised: 'If I ever find out you're lying, I'll kill you.' And Angie knew he meant it.

Den arranged for a second honeymoon in Venice where they, by chance, bumped into Jan. So when Den overheard a drunken Angie confess to a barman on the Orient Express on the way home that she had been lying ('I told my husband I was dying, and now I wish I was'), it made him want Jan even more.

But not before he'd taught Angie a lesson. He was going to do worse than kill her, he was going to take away everything that mattered to her; the Vic, Sharon and her job. He was going to divorce her, and she would be the last to know. While Angie carried on with the pretence of dying, Den carried on with the pretence of being married, meanwhile consulting a solicitor.

And on Christmas Day 1986, Den gave Angie a present neither she, nor anyone else in Albert Square, would ever forget – a divorce petition.

As she stormed out of the pub with Sharon in tow, she made sure she was in full view of the punters so they too could see what a dirty rat he really was.

Jan was moved into the Vic by Den and she tried – and failed – to fill Angie's shoes. She was useless behind the bar and even more useless at serving the regulars. Profits plummeted and Angie couldn't have been happier. Even Den had to admit that the Vic just wasn't the Vic without Angie's 100-watt smile. So she came back to work where she belonged.

And she still sparkled, still turned on the charm, and was as tactile as ever, constantly pinching the cheek of a cute lad, and hugging a girlfriend in need of a pick-me-up. Angie's hospitality was always on the house.

She had amazing reserves for dealing with – and hiding – pain. She'd slap on her 'war paint', down a G&T and be 'Good ol' Ange' all over again. While Den brooded in the background (behind his legendary stony stare he fretted about Michelle and Vicki), Angie was the professional masochist.

The day their decree absolute came through in May

19

1987, Angie joined Den for an after-hours champagne toast. But the poignant moment was interrupted when Mags, Den's new girlfriend, came by looking for company. Angie realised he would never change and left to be manageress at a new rival pub, the Dagmar.

But even though she got to wear smarter suits and ruled her own roost, the Dagmar's yuppie customers with their pretentious West End manner finally got to her, and yet again she returned to the Vic. Although this time it was strictly business – she and Den were to be partners – Sharon always hoped it would be more.

The year 1988 got off to a bad start for the Wattses as Angie was admitted to hospital with kidney failure. After months of avoiding it, Den finally visited his ex-wife in hospital where they made plans about starting over in a new pub. But first, Angie said, she wanted a holiday in Spain. Her escort for the trip was actually one of Den's best mates, Sonny, who ran another local pub, the Feathers, with his wife Ree.

Sonny had been visiting Angie in hospital and they had fallen for each other, and in May they left the Square together in a cab bound for the airport – and a new life in Marbella. (Angie would later leave Spain and Sonny for Florida, where she remarried.)

Den let the tenancy of the Vic go to Pat and Frank, and the Firm (it was always known that Den had gangster connections) put him up in business at Strokes Wine Bar in Turpin Road. Strokes, unsurprisingly, was just an outlet for money-laundering.

Reinforcing the adage that the East End looks after its own, Den made sure the Dagmar was torched to the ground after good friend Kathy Beale was raped there by James Willmott-Brown.

The Firm later asked Den to take the rap for the crime, so he went into hiding. But after the police had been tipped off, he voluntarily gave himself up and was banged up on remand at Dickens Hill prison until February 1989.

En route to his trial, Den was kidnapped by the Firm, who wanted to stop him from testifying against them, but he escaped. Desperate to speak to an ally, he tried to contact Michelle, the only person who still respected him and whom he trusted to keep a secret. They arranged to meet at their old haunt, the canal.

But the Firm, suspicious of Michelle's interest in Den, followed her, and after Den and Michelle had said their goodbyes and parted, Den was shot by a gangster concealing his gun in a bunch of daffodils.

A year later, a body that could have been Den's was dragged out of the canal, but the identity of the corpse was never proved beyond doubt.

Den lives on in Vicki, and something of Angie remains in the Square thanks to Sharon, who has become an equally vibrant, younger version of her mum. One way or another, this pair will never be forgotten.

MICHELLE AND SHARON

Michelle and Sharon have both grown up to be like their mothers. But while Sharon is repeating the pattern, Michelle is struggling to break the mould.

From play school these two East End daughters have been best friends, their lives uniquely intertwined, sharing secrets like most girls share lipsticks.

Although Michelle isn't quite a year older than Sharon, she always seemed more mature. She wasn't preoccupied with boys, and she understood the value of a good education.

Sharon however, although smart (she ended up with five O levels, one of which was grade A), was a ditsy teenager constantly dressed in pink fluffy jumpers. And her parents, Den and Angie Watts, indirectly encouraged her to do daft things by either ignoring her or palming her off with a tenner.

Money never came so easily for Michelle in the Fowler household. For years she had to share a bedroom with her parents, Pauline and Arthur, separated from them only by a curtain. It was only when her troubled brother Mark ran away that she finally got a room of her own.

If local gambler Ali Osman had run a book on which of the two girls would have gotten pregnant as a teenager, Sharon would have got shorter odds. But while she treated her virginity like a burden, propositioning Michelle's boyfriend Kelvin in the launderette ('I'll go on the pill,' she offered), Michelle had already, secretly, lost her virginity – and was pregnant.

Just after her little brother Martin was born, and Arthur had started a new job, Michelle felt ignored, especially by her dad, and she went looking for paternal understanding with neighbours Ali, Tony, Andy and Den.

Scared and confused by her expectant state, Michelle didn't know what to do. Gingerly she confided in her gran, Lou Beale, who relished the role of wise old woman but was concerned for Michelle and arranged for a pregnancy test, which was positive.

The next step was to tell Pauline. Michelle took the plunge while Pauline was doing the ironing. Her creases were so perfect it was as if she hadn't heard what Michelle had said.

While Pauline organised a family conference – a long-standing tradition at number 45 – Michelle stole her keys to the launderette and snuck in to phone the father in secret.

'Thank God it's you,' she said into the receiver. 'I'm pregnant and you're the father.' And she arranged to meet him at the canal at 12.30 the next day.

No wonder she was keeping the father's identity a secret – it was Sharon's dad Den! They walked solemnly along the canal, his dog Roly leading the way.

It was revealed that they'd made love in the saloon bar of the Queen Victoria one night in August. She'd gone over to the Vic to collect some cassettes from Sharon and on her way out she had bumped into Den locking up. He invited her to stay for a drink and a chat, and one thing had obviously led to another.

Den told Michelle that he wouldn't leave his wife, Angie, but he would make sure that she was taken care of. To protect Angie, and especially Sharon, they vowed to keep their fling a secret.

When Michelle told Sharon that she was pregnant, Sharon's reaction was 'What was it like?' She was still more interested in sex than anything else. Oblivious to the irony, Angie warmly congratulated Michelle on her news, and the Square prepared for another arrival while Sharon and Michelle swotted for their O levels.

Sharon, along with Ian and Kelvin, formed a pop group with Kelvin's socialist friends from college, Harry and

Tessa. They agreed that the band, Dog Market, would build up a following with middle-of-the-road pop before hitting their fans with their political message!

Sharon arranged for the would-be pop stars to play their first gig at the Queen Vic. But before they'd got through the first song, Venus, the sound equipment blew the electrical circuit in the pub. Den banned them from his establishment and the group re-named themselves The Banned.

While Sharon and The Banned prepared for a talent quest at the local community centre, Michelle was being proposed to.

Lofty, persuaded by Wicksy's comment that no one would have her now, had decided that Michelle and her unborn baby needed someone to take care of them. And he wanted to be the one to do the caring. His life had been empty since he'd been forced to leave the army due to dormant asthma. His only living relative was his aunty Irene, and this was the perfect way of creating his own family. He knew Michelle didn't love him – she was still carrying a torch for Den – but he hoped that in time she would learn to love him.

But Michelle politely turned him down. However, Lofty persisted and eventually, in April 1986, she said yes. Sharon meanwhile had started seeing 'Chelle's cousin Ian, and from the way she acted you'd have thought it was *Romeo and Juliet II*. Although it clearly wasn't, everyone's readiness to ridicule her about it made her feel insecure.

While Michelle became the centre of attention, Sharon was ignored. Arthur fretted over how to pay for the impending nuptials. Lofty worried about everything (although Den took care of the engagement ring, on the grounds that Michelle never found out where it came from), and Michelle, heavily pregnant and unsure of the future, was in no mood for Sharon's distinctly teenage chatterings.

Even Den was more worried about Michelle than he was about Sharon. So it should have come as no surprise that Sharon ran away. Angie feared the worst, but her daughter was actually hiding out at Mary's. It was Ethel who finally twigged Sharon's whereabouts after she'd spotted Ian visiting Mary's more times than was friendly, and she persuaded Sharon to return to the Vic.

In May 1986, Michelle gave birth to Vicki Louise Fowler. After the assorted Fowlers had left mother and baby for a good night's rest, Den tricked his way on to the ward pretending to be Michelle's godfather. She handed him little Vicki. 'Go on,' she said. 'I want you to hold her. She's yours too.'

Den asked the name of his only natural child. 'Vicki.' Michelle tried to explain: 'Well, my granddad was Albert . . .' but Den knew the Victoria she was named after was his pub. It was to be one of the few times he ever held his daughter.

Sharon was to be Michelle's bridesmaid. But although she could get Michelle to the church, she couldn't get her down the aisle, and Michelle jilted Lofty – a crushing blow for the sweet young man.

Michelle eventually married Lofty in a registrar's office and they moved into his flat above Dr Legg's.

Sharon may have had a slower journey to adulthood, but she was getting there. She had a serious relationship with Wicksy, but couldn't bring herself to sleep with him. On her eighteenth birthday, she went to church – part of her search for some stability in her life – and met Duncan, a curate. They went out for a while, but he couldn't bring himself to sleep with her.

Michelle meanwhile was pregnant again, this time by Lofty. His joy turned to unbearable heartache when she confessed that she'd had the baby aborted. He threw her out and called her selfish – a criticism that has often been levelled at Michelle – and he soon left Walford altogether.

Sharon and Michelle both embarked on a series of dead-end jobs, from hairdresser to travel agent, and they both squeezed in some dead-end relationships as well. While Michelle dated a series of older men (looking for Den's replacement?) Sharon finally lost her virginity – to

Wicksy, after all. She was crushed when he left her for Cindy.

One of the many things Sharon and Michelle had in common was their love for Den. They both kept him on a pedestal because he took care of things no one else could. (Neither of them seemed to realise that without him they'd never have been in trouble in the first place.) So when Den was killed it was a painful and confusing time for both of them. They were sharing a flat at the time (the flat Den had bought them at 43a Albert Square), and Michelle felt that they had enough private space for her to tell Sharon about Den. Vicki had been brought up to call Sharon 'Daddy Sharon', and Michelle thought her best friend would be comforted by the fact that there really was a family tie.

She was wrong. Sharon ran away in tears feeling betrayed by her closest pal and her adored daddy. But once the girls had made up, their friendship became even closer and it is impossible to imagine what could possibly threaten their friendship ever again.

Michelle started university and Sharon started seeing local mechanic Grant Mitchell. Although his older brother Phil was the nicer guy, Sharon liked the bastard in Grant; perhaps she too was looking for another Den.

Sharon had also started looking for her natural parents, but when she came face to face with Carol Hanley it was a disappointment for both of them. Carol and her husband Ron had just had a baby and she felt that Sharon would only rock the boat. After a few difficult meetings, Sharon realised that she didn't need her natural mother, but she felt content that she had seen her at last.

When Grant arranged a surprise wedding for Sharon on Boxing Day 1991, Sharon didn't know what to say, so she turned to Michelle for advice.

'Do you love him?' Michelle asked. And that was all Sharon needed to know and she agreed to marry Grant – on the grounds that he got her the Vic. That meant brother Phil's financial involvement and the three of them became equal partners in the pub.

But they were to become unequal partners in love when Sharon could contain her feelings for Phil no more, and started a passionate clandestine affair with him. While Grant was in prison she and Phil lived like man and wife, but when Grant was released, she chose Grant with little consideration of Phil. This time it was Sharon's turn to be called selfish. To this day Grant doesn't know about the affair – but if he ever found out, he'd surely kill them both.

Michelle, too, lives in fear that Vicki will be taken from her again as she was in March 1993, when she was kidnapped from outside the school gates. At the time of the kidnap, Michelle was being hounded by a fellow student, Jack Woodman, with whom she'd had a one-night stand. But when Jack – who was mentally unstable – decided he wanted more, he terrorised Michelle by turning up on her doorstep at all hours, becoming friends with her flatmate Rachel, and making unsettling phone calls.

So when Vicki disappeared on 4 March, Jack was Michelle's number one suspect. As it turned out, the culprit who had put Michelle through the most harrowing days of her life was a childless housewife, Audrey Whittingham, who wanted to 'borrow' Vicki for a while.

Although Sharon and Michelle have grown up just yards away from each other, and shared more traumas than can be remembered, these two women remain very different. When they go out together, blonde Sharon will pile on the warpaint and step into a mini skirt (just like her mum), but Michelle will still undersell herself, letting her brown hair remain lifeless, and looking embarrassed in anything dressier than a pair of jeans.

But these two East End darlings are where they belong. Sharon is entrenched behind the bar at the Queen Victoria, flirting and gossiping with the punters just like Angie. The pub is very precious to Sharon – it's been her home all her life – and she belongs there. She'll fight for the Queen Victoria pub like Scarlett O'Hara fought for Tara.

And Michelle too still lives under the umbrella of her

historic family. She's so like her mother – a survivor –
even though she sometimes gets scared that one day she
won't be able to live up to her genes. She's determined to
make something better of her life – for herself, and for
Vicki.

And one way or another Vicki is going to be well
provided for. Her tough mother will instil in her the East
End values she holds dear, and her adoring big sister will
make sure she wants for nothing.

DOT AND NICK COTTON

Dot Cotton was the closest thing Albert Square will ever have to a saint, and her son Nick was Walford's own original sinner.

Dot's happiest days were during the war when she was evacuated at the age of four to Wales. Where, for the first time, she wasn't a burden to her Walford family. That was the only time in her life when she knew continued happiness.

At the end of the war, she was moved back to the East End where her home life was never secure. Her parents split and remarried and she was presented with a half-sister, Rose.

So when charming Charlie Cotton told her he loved her, she didn't know any better and married him when she was only twenty. At 21 she was pregnant – and delighted. But Charlie was adamantly opposed to the baby and used all his charm to persuade Dot to have an abortion. And, to her continuing shame and heartache, she did.

Charlie left her for the first time shortly afterwards, and for the rest of her life he would keep turning up on her doorstep whenever he was down on his luck. And, charitable soul that she was, she would always take him in. You see, Dot is a devout Christian who can quote verses from the Bible like a vicar, even though her references are often totally inappropriate!

But no matter how tragic her own life was at times, Dot would never stop relishing sticking her nose into someone else's problems. Dot was, is, and always will be an incurable gossip. She also suffers from incurable hypochondria!

If it wasn't for her faith in God, Dot could not have endured some of the heartache in her life. The revelation that Charlie had been carrying on with her half-sister Rose for years was nothing compared to the fact that he was a bigamist! He had also married a woman called Joan Leggett in the Midlands. And Joan, like Dot, must also have wondered why his long-distance lorry deliveries took months, even years, to complete. Charlie was absent so often that he didn't meet his son until Nick was well into his twenties.

Dot prayed that one day the Charlie she had fallen for would come home. He never did; he just got better at abusing her kindness.

But no matter how much praying Dot did, she never quite forgave herself for producing Nick. Where Charlie was pathetic and lazy, Nick was cunning and had pure evil running through his veins. Burglary, pimping, blackmail and murder: Nick Cotton committed them all – and never showed any remorse.

With an absent father and a mother who thought he was the golden child, Nick had no one to correct him when he went astray. And the older he got, the more ruthless he became – but he would never hurt his 'Ma', and she always faithfully defended him.

When Nick was in the frame for murdering Reg Cox in 1985 – he battered the old man, stole his war medals and left him to die, but was never convicted – Dot was upset by the locals condemning him before he'd even been arrested, and her holier-than-thou attitude won her few friends.

But she had to eat humble pie when she herself was arrested for shoplifting a year later. She claimed a menopausal hot flush had sent her doolally momentarily. Dot delayed getting medical help for her 'change of life' because Dr Legg was away and his locum was an Indian.

Dot and Nick were both racists – she out of ignorance, he out of venom. But Dr Singh put Dot on HRT, and his tender care helped Dot slowly change her opinion on immigrants. Her prejudices also ran to homosexuality, and when she discovered that Colin and Barry at number 3 shared the same sheets she practically fainted with revulsion. She thought they were sinful and told Barry that God had sent AIDS to punish them. 'Why then,' asked Barry, 'are lesbians least at risk?' She had no answer, and no answers either for any of her petty warped conceptions, and eventually Colin became one of her closest friends in Albert Square.

Nick, however, never tried to change his opinions. As far as he was concerned, 'fairies' (as he called them) were just other people to pick on.

He tried blackmailing Colin at one point – he knew Barry was under 21 – but Colin stood up to him and even threw a few punches himself.

Kathy Beale put up no such defence when he black-mailed her in 1985. Nick had broken into Dr Legg's surgery looking for drugs to sell (Nick himself was a former addict), but had stumbled across Kathy's medical records which stated she had had a kid at fourteen. He threatened to tell her husband unless she paid him money, which she did until she broke down and revealed that she had been raped and given birth to a daughter she'd had adopted.

When the men of the Square found out Nick had been extorting money from her and threatening her, they lynched him. He was forced to leave Walford with his tail between his legs, but everyone knew he would be back.

Dot always worried about where Nick went when he was out of her sight, but like his father, he too had a secret 'other' family.

He had fathered a son, Ashley, and intermittently he went to stay with him and his mother at their place in Poplar. Nick never told Dot about her grandson because he didn't want her to have anything new to interfere in.

While Nick was away, Dot busied herself with other people's gossip puffing on her ever-present fag and saying, 'Ooh, I say.' She became as much part of Albert Square as Pete's fruit and veg stall and the café's stewed tea. She provided the locals with humour, advice and the best service wash in East London!

Her floral print nylon blouses and her lacquered hair became a trade mark. Dot was never to be seen in a pair of slacks – that wouldn't have been proper.

When she wasn't in the Bridge Street Launderette where she worked eavesdropping, she was sitting in the Vic with Ethel and Lou, supping her tomato juice and complaining about whatever she could.

Although Dot could be relied upon to pass on even the most trivial piece of tittle-tattle, she could also be trusted to keep a secret. Sharon would often turn to her for advice when she was a teenager, and she was the only person (excluding family) that Kathy told that Donna was her daughter.

Dot saw herself as a pillar of the community, a sort of disciple leading the unconverted, and she saw it as her Christian duty to organise the local Neighbourhood Watch scheme. The other residents of Albert Square just saw it as a way for her to legitimise her snooping. But the truth was she really did care about the community she had grown up in, and she really cared about the people too.

Over the years she took in plenty of waifs and strays – Rod, Donna, Disa – and she prayed for them all.

Good fortune finally came her way in March 1990 when she won £10,000 on the bingo. It came as no surprise that as soon as she was presented with the cheque, Nick resurfaced in Walford. But this time, he swore, he had changed. To his mother's delight he had found God, and he said he wanted to make up for all the pain he had caused her. He became the dutiful son, taking care of his Ma and making meals for her. Dot, of course, was taken in.

But behind Nick's sweet façade was a heart of calculating malice: he still wore his too-tight trousers and his perma-sneer; and his uncanny eagerness to cook Dot's meals masked his intention to slowly poison her – and inherit her winnings.

The 'special diet' he claimed he had prepared for her would cure her never ending migraines, he said. But instead of curing her, it just made her more sick.

When Charlie found the poison, the police were called, but Dot – revived from the brink of death – refused to press charges. Yet again Nick had escaped justice.

Dot sensibly changed her will, but she was distraught that Nick could be so callous. She had always believed that deep down he loved her, but now she had sadly been proved wrong.

The next sighting of Nick was in Dickens Hill prison – inside for a minor offence – where he confessed to Den that he had indeed killed Reg Cox. It was another year before he dared show his face in Albert Square, and what a face it was. Red eyes and a haggard stare with a five-day growth, it was obvious from looking at him that he had rediscovered heroin. Shortly after Nick's arrival, Dot learnt that Charlie had been killed in a road accident.

In her grief, Dot found the charity to help Nick – he had always known that she wouldn't turn him away. And so with the help of Pete Beale, Dot locked Nick in his room, sealed the windows and forced him to go cold turkey in an attempt to beat his addiction. What Pete and Dot didn't realise was that Nick had managed to sneak a knife into his makeshift cell. From his window Nick saw Clyde Tavernier, knife in hand, standing over the body of publican Eddie Royle in the Square, and he gave this 'evidence' to the police.

However, after the case against Clyde disintegrated, Nick confessed to Dot that he had escaped from his room and killed Royle. Dot could not defend her son any longer, and she shopped him to the police.

Nick was surprised at his mum's actions – he never thought she'd turn against him – but he had hurt her too many times and she would not let him get away with murder. She might have been frail and weak, but she could still teach her son a lesson.

At the trial, Dot testified emotionally against her son (it was obviously tearing her apart), but her evidence was not enough to convict him. So yet again his evil had escaped the law.

Dot thought, and maybe even hoped, that she had seen the last of her son, so disgusted was she with the monster she had created. And it seemed Nick was finally out of the picture, and that meant that he was now living full time with his son Ashley and girlfriend Zoe.

Convinced that Nick was now a reformed character, Zoe decided to make contact with Dot so that Ashley could get to know his grandma. At first Dot didn't want to know as she had been conned by Hazel years ago that she was a Gran. But Zoe persisted and soon introduced Dot to her real grandchild. And they got on famously – for once a deed of Nick's failed to bring her misery. She treated Ashley to the things Nick and Zoe couldn't afford, and Ashley was the ray of sunshine that had been missing in Dot's life for so long.

So when Ashley asked her to take care of him full-time, it was an easy decision to make. Dot left Walford to be a professional gran in 1993 – and Albert Square has never been the same since!

THE MITCHELL BROTHERS

Phil Mitchell and his brother Grant are what the East End is all about. They're rough, tough and ready to throw the first punch.

They swaggered into Albert Square in February 1991 bringing with them their traditional attitudes to women, boozing, and crime. (They both have criminal records, Phil for nothing more serious than drunk and disorderly, Grant for assault.) And Grant in particular had a sense of menace about him, like he could explode at any minute.

When he does lash out (which is quite often), big brother Phil is there to diffuse the situation and soothe his brother's temper.

Their background is typical of the East End. Their dad Eric was a professional boxer (both sons have inherited his physical build) who married their mum Peggy only because she was pregnant with Phil.

As they grew up, many of their friends became crooks, giving the Mitchells a direct line to local gangsters. Grant thinks this is very glamorous and sometimes acts as if the Krays are still ruling the roost.

To escape some of his villainous friends for a while, Grant enlisted in the army. He was posted to Cyprus where he was in the Paras. In 1982, war was declared in the Falklands and Grant was sent to fight. Combat affected him deeply; he killed several men and watched his closest friends die. Unsurprisingly, this left him psychologically deeply scarred, and for years he was haunted by nightmares and prone to violent rages. These aggressive outbursts led people to judge him harshly, as they masked his softer side which he rarely lets people see.

When Sharon put her flat at 43a up for sale, Grant decided to buy it. Their negotiations over the sale caused them to spend more time than was necessary together, and it was clear they had fallen in love.

Maybe it was because he was jealous, but Phil could never bring himself to be really happy for Grant and Sharon. Phil needed a girlfriend, but he was notoriously unlucky in love. When he finally did meet a girl he could care for, Anne, it turned out she was married.

Like any East End lad, Grant has his manor, his turf, and if that's invaded he flips. He wanders round like a predatory ape in a Lacoste shirt ready for a rumble. So when landlord Eddie Royle started flirting with Sharon, it was only a matter of time before Grant 'taught him a lesson'. He beat up Eddie so badly that he required brain surgery. Grant, too, could have used a bit of help with his brain. But short of a lobotomy nothing can change his 'fight now, don't bother to think later' attitude.

However, this time even Grant was shocked by the power of his bare hands. He hadn't meant to land Eddie in hospital, but he'd lost control – the demons from the war were obviously still with him. Grant retreated inside himself, barely speaking to Phil, let alone anyone else. But Phil had seen Grant like this before and knew to let him be. Sharon, in all her days in the Queen Vic, had never seen anything like it. She was scared by Grant, angry at him for attacking Eddie, but also concerned. The events proved to her that she really did love him, and really did want to help him.

But Grant had his own therapy – to re-enlist. Sharon begged him not to, but Grant wanted to go back because only other soldiers could understand what he had gone through. Although he passed the physical with flying colours, the army wouldn't accept him on the grounds that he was psychologically unfit.

The brothers Mitchell run their own motor-repair shop underneath the railway arches off Turpin Road, and they can fix far more than a gear box. Need a driving licence in a hurry? A car log book? An MOT on a rust heap?

Well Phil and Grant will see you right – for a price. They may not be Nick Cotton, but they're certainly not beyond stretching the law. These boys have connections that can see to almost anything. Fake ID, a safe house – they could probably even arrange for an enemy to be bumped off, although Phil's conscience would no doubt stop them.

Mercifully Phil has enough morals for the both of them, so when Mark Fowler was charged for couriering stolen log books, Phil stepped in to take the blame. Thanks to their dad, the lads also have contacts in the powerful East End boxing circuit, and once rigged a couple of fights for Clyde Tavernier.

They took Ricky Butcher on as an apprentice mechanic at the arches, because he was dirt cheap and too dim-witted to mind fetching the tea from the cafe. What they didn't bank on though was Ricky falling for their fifteen-year-old sister Samantha.

Sam had been having trouble with her mum's boyfriend Kevin, and stayed a couple of nights in the workshop. When her big brothers found out they weren't happy, but they were furious when they learnt that Ricky had been the one letting her in.

Phil and Grant were so opposed to Ricky seeing their kid sis that Sam took to meeting her beau in secret. Everyone else's opposition to their romance made Sam and Ricky more determined to stay together. So determined, in fact, that they eloped to Gretna Green.

What 'thicky Ricky' forgot to take with them on their journey to Scotland was the RAC route map he'd ordered, and as soon as Phil discovered this piece of evidence, he and his brother were hot on the young lovers' trail. When they got to Gretna Green there was no sign of Sam and Ricky, but Grant decided not to waste the trip and booked a date for him and Sharon. However, despite her brothers' attempts, Sam still managed to marry Ricky.

Sharon accepted Grant's unexpected proposal and he was over the moon. No matter what else he would ever say or do to Sharon, there could be no doubt that he truly loved her – even if he wasn't very good at saying so.

Their wedding plans had to be put on ice while Sharon took on the temporary tenancy of the Vic after Eddie Royle's murder, and in a way Sharon was relieved, as things had been moving a little too quickly for her. But Grant couldn't wait to make his beautiful girlfriend his wife, and he arranged a secret wedding for Boxing Day as a Christmas present. Sharon was shocked, but decided the wedding was only sooner rather than later and so she agreed to marry him on the grounds that he got her the Vic.

That required money – and Grant didn't have enough. Brother Phil was persuaded to sell his flat and put up a third of the money for the pub, making him an equal partner in their new home.

As Grant's traditional values towards his wife surfaced, Sharon found a stronger and stronger bond forming between her and his gentle brother. Phil was the only other person to have lived with Grant's moods and he was able to offer Sharon much sympathy.

Grant was desperate to be a father (it was another chance to assert his masculinity) but Sharon felt she was too young to become a mum. But his manner scared her so much that she couldn't tell him she was still taking the Pill. When she finally told him to spite him, he overreacted and reminded Sharon once again of the violent temper she had married.

Grant became even moodier and would stay out all hours, come back drunk when he felt like it and sincerely believed he could make up for his behaviour with a bunch of flowers and a 'Sorry, darlin''.

One night when Grant was out very late boozing with his mates, Sharon and Phil cleaned up after closing but could contain their feelings for each other no more. They embraced and kissed passionately, knocking over glasses in their haste to get upstairs. After they had made love, they heard Grant come in drunk and so they got up to talk to him. But neither of them could bring themselves to confess their sin, so Phil told her, 'If you go to bed with Grant now, that's it.' Sharon, in her second moment of weakness that night, chose Grant.

About that time, Grant's mates in the Firm asked him if he could supply a car-and-wheels man – a getaway driver – for a bank job. In return he'd get a cut of the loot. But the driver Grant hired did a runner with all the booty and the Firm held Grant responsible.

They heavied him for the money, and Grant – backed into a corner – decided to take drastic action. He planned to torch Sharon's precious pub and claim the insurance money.

His convenient alibi was a party over the Square where he'd been seen by several witnesses all evening. He slipped out for a moment, dashed back across the Square and lit a fire in the saloon bar before returning to the party. What he didn't know was that Sharon was upstairs, crying her eyes out after a fight with Phil when he'd called her selfish for ignoring his feelings.

When Sharon's shouts for help were heard from inside the inferno, both brothers had reason to feel guilty. But even guilt couldn't turn Grant into a perfect husband, and after accusing his wife of having somebody else (which she denied) he confessed, out of spite, that he had been responsible for the fire at the Queen Vic.

That was the final straw and Sharon told Grant that their marriage was over and she wanted him out. But it's difficult to walk when you're digging your heels in, and Grant counter-attacked with a threat to sell the Vic from under her. He thought he could count on his brother's complicity, but he was unaware of Phil's illicit loyalty to Sharon.

Phil had been put in a terrible position by the two people he loved most, and so he played his trump card and refused to do anything. They would have to make the decision, he said, not him.

Well if Phil wasn't going to do anything, Sharon was ready for action. She packed her bags and left for a holiday with her mum in Florida. After all, they couldn't sell the Vic without her signature, and if she wasn't in the country she couldn't sign a thing.

Grant and Phil muddled through until her return, but nothing had really changed. Grant still didn't trust her and she was still scared of him. And she had a right to be – it wasn't long before he hit her. Although she tried to cover up the bruise, Michelle twigged that something was wrong. And so the next time she thought Grant was going to be violent towards her mate she called the police.

When the Bill arrived Grant was livid, and he attacked one of the coppers – but not before he'd managed to bloody Michelle's nose. The magistrate held Grant on remand for assaulting a police officer, a godsend for Phil and Sharon who at last were able to live together as man and wife.

Phil visited his brother in jail, and Grant asked if Sharon had another fella. Naturally he couldn't bring himself to tell Grant the truth. Sharon chickened out of the dirty deed too when Grant cried and said, 'The thought of you is the only thing that is keeping me sane.'

So when he was let out, the *menage à trois* was still as volatile as ever, only now Grant really seemed to have changed. And yet again, when faced with an ultimatum, Sharon chose to be with her husband. But there was always just an element of doubt that she only chose Grant because that meant keeping her Queen Vic.

To show his commitment to the marriage, Grant gave up working at the Arches, and Phil was happy to spend more time there – anything to keep him away from watching Sharon and Grant paw over each other at the Vic.

Phil felt pretty sorry for himself, so when he met Russian immigrant Nadia in a wine bar in Southampton and listened to her tales of persecution, he felt guilty for moping around and decided to help her. He would marry her so she could become a British citizen and avoid deportation. Finally Phil, who was always so unlucky with relationships, had tied the knot. If only it had been for love.

But just when he was about to give up on finding the girl of his dreams, he discovered she had been under his nose all along. Kathy Beale had always given him extra chips with his fry-up in the café, but he hadn't realised she had an ulterior motive. But then neither did she. It took a romantic weekend in Paris for Kathy and Phil to realise what they had. After a stroll along the banks of the Seine wrapped up in each other's arms they agreed to be straight with each other without promising an exchange of rings. Phil even told her about Sharon.

They had a couple of blissful months together before Kathy found out Phil had been keeping a huge secret from her – the fact that he was married! Kathy was hurt and horrified, but she understood his motives. And anyway she fancied him rotten.

But when Phil had to live with Nadia to fool the Home Office, things became strained. He managed to convince Kathy that he didn't fancy Nadia and never had done, he was just simply doing her a favour. Nadia, however, was beginning to see she had a chance at happiness with Phil. After all, compared to what she had known, Phil lived like a king. Nadia made it her business to make Kathy feel insecure – if she could get Kath out of the picture her future was secure.

On Christmas Day, after typical Albert Square festive activities and the requisite over-consumption of alcohol, Nadia finally lured Phil into bed to consummate their marriage. When Nadia told Kathy that she had 'gone to bed' with Phil, Kath was so fed up with her meddling that she ignored what she perceived as bragging.

Nevertheless the damage had been done, and even if Phil could keep his betrayal secret from his girlfriend, he knew that once again he had unforgivably lied to Kathy.

But even deceit can't take away from the fact that these two are made for each other. After all, they even have matching denim shirts!

THE BUTCHERS

Like a lot of East End women, Pat Butcher is as tough as the old boots unlucky fishermen drag out of the canal. She's been there, seen it, done it, got the gold lamé embossed T-shirt and now she's mellowed. But it was a long, hard journey to happiness for the brassiest woman east of Whitechapel market.

Pat Harris grew up kicking around the streets of Walford with the likes of Angie Watts. They were pretty girls and got a lot of attention from the fellas, but Angie was saving herself for Den Watts, a local rascal with the cutest DA in town.

When Pat was sixteen, she won Miss Butlins at the holiday camp in Clacton in 1958, and a certain Frank Butcher was in the audience with his fiancée June. Frank was so enamoured with the beauty queen he had just seen that he made his excuses to June and went to Pat's chalet with her where they made love. Pat later confessed that this was her first time.

Frank told Pat that he loved her, but he wouldn't leave June because she was pregnant. Frank and June eventually had four children together, Clare, Ricky, Diane and Janine, who was only four when her mother died. Pat meanwhile had gone looking for the affection Frank denied her and was branded a slut, although that didn't stop the local lads from sleeping with her. In fact about the only boy in Walford who resisted her offers was Arthur Fowler. She still continued to see Frank Butcher, and every now and then they'd sneak away for a weekend. Pat loved her time with Frank because he knew her as a virginal teenager, not a middle-aged whore, and consequently treated her right.

It wasn't long before Pat thought she was pregnant and married the 'father', Pete Beale. Although this proved a false alarm they stayed together and had a son, David. When Pat got pregnant for real, she knew that the child she was carrying might not be Pete's. She had also been carrying on with Pete's brother Kenny, a guy she fancied called Brian Wicks, and Den. But Pat needed a father for her kids, and if Pete was dumb enough to offer . . .

The marriage was doomed to failure even after the birth of little Simon. For starters, Pete's mum Lou hated her. Lou knew of Pat's reputation as a scarlet woman, and she also believed that Pat was trapping and using her adored son. She'd also guessed about the relationship with Kenny. So with formidable Lou pushing weak Pete to make the break, it wasn't long before Pat's misbehaviour led Pete to leave her.

By now, Pat couldn't survive without men – tarting was a way of life to her – and she married Brian Wicks on the rebound. Brian adopted Pat's sons and brought them up as his own so Pat stayed with him out of loyalty way after the marriage was really over. The years with Brian took their toll on Pat.

He used to drink heavily and occasionally would hit her; she lost her pride and lost her looks and she nearly lost her sons. David had little contact with his mother for years, and Wicksy (Simon) left Pat to be with the man he thought was his dad, Pete. (Wicksy had another reason for fleeing to Albert Square – loan sharks were after him for £1,500.)

Eventually Pat plucked up the courage to leave Brian, and she followed her son to Albert Square where she found a room and a job at the Vic with her old mates Den and Angie. 'Fat Pat', as they called her, was a big hit with most of the punters – as long as they were men. But her flirting embarrassed Wicksy who was also working behind the bar. The pint-buyers loved her flash clothes from the market, her platinum hair and her well-displayed cleavage, and the rift between mother and son grew wider as a result. But Pat wasn't going to be bullied by her son, and she continued to see as many men as she could. In fact at one time, some of the regulars suspected she was on the game.

Unsurprisingly, Pat's arrival in Albert Square upset the fruit and veg cart for Pete and his family. The revelations about Wicksy's paternity didn't help, and neither did Pat's comments about Pete's performance in bed. 'I could fit it all on the back of a fag packet,' she claimed.

So when Pat became the latest victim of the 'Walford Attacker' Pete was the number one suspect, especially as he didn't have an alibi for any of the other attacks.

Life took an unexpected upturn for Pat in February 1988 when she met Frank for lunch during one of the Vic's Ladies Darts team's outings. His wife had died, he said, and now he was free to marry her.

They were an odd couple and it was hard to see what they saw in each other – the years hadn't been kind to either of them. Frank was a balding car salesman with word perfect banter, and slightly too small suit to match his Meccano glasses. Pat's waistline had tripled since they'd first met, and her blonde hair now came straight from the bottle.

Pat had reason to be suspicious of Frank's intentions after all these years, and worried that he only wanted a mother for his children. But he made her feel sixteen again, he didn't treat her like a slut, and so she said 'yes' and they tied the knot in June 1989.

The wedding was a traditional East End bash with jellied eels and a good old knees-up round the piano. After the honeymoon, it was back to life in the Queen Victoria where Mr and Mrs Butcher were now landlords. They also called the shots in a few other establishments in Walford as Frank became a silent partner in the café with Pauline and Kathy, and owner of the car lot. When he also bought the B&B off Doris, the Butchers realised they were over-stretching their resources and let the Vic tenancy go.

Things may have been going well businesswise, but there was trouble brewing on the home front. Janine had not taken to Pat as a stepmum and Mo had not taken to her as a daughter-in-law. Ricky couldn't care less – he was more interested in girls (he had flings with Marie the hairdresser and Shireen Karim), but Diane was starting to feel the strain and ran away.

Frank was desolate and he combed the streets of London looking for his little princess. But he had to wait three months before Diane made contact, and even when she did return home it was obvious she wasn't going to hang around for long.

Mark Fowler's reappearance in his home town was a significant event for the Butchers. Not only did he save Mo from a fire which she'd started herself through absent-mindedness, but he also fell in love with Diane and it was to her that he first revealed he was HIV positive.

The fire was the turning point for Mo, and Frank could no longer ignore his mother's memory lapses. It came as little surprise when she was diagnosed as a sufferer of Alzheimer's.

Pat and Frank decided that they would try and take care of her; after all they had a spare room now newlywed Ricky was squatting with wife Sam across the Square. But Mo's condition deteriorated and she needed more care than the Butchers could offer, so it was agreed that she would go and live with Frank's big sister Joan in Essex.

Christmas 1992 was a terrible time for the Butchers of Walford. Not only had they been forced to sell the B&B due to the recession and move into a pokey flat (43b), but Frank hadn't heard from Diane for months (the last he'd heard was that she'd been grape-picking in France) and he was disappointed when she didn't return for a traditional turkey dinner. Sam and Ricky were obviously heading for the divorce court. Sam had met a West End toff called Clive who told her she could do better than Albert Square and Ricky. She believed him and had started to shut Ricky out while she embarked on a modelling career.

Joan called to tell Frank that his mum had died, but he had no time to mourn as Pat was about to endure the toughest time of her life. On Christmas Eve, while doing a job for her cab firm, PatCabs, she ran over a young woman. Pat had only had a couple of festive G&Ts, but when she couldn't get another driver for a valued customer, she took the fare herself.

She was numb. She felt ashamed and didn't want to leave the house, unless it was to visit the hospital to see how the girl, Stephanie Watson, was doing. When the news came through that she had died, Pat clammed up with guilt.

Frank did his best to alleviate the pain and ease her back into their daily life, but Pat railed against his attempts to get her back behind the wheel.

Her best therapy was coming face to face with Stephanie's mum. Mrs Watson told how Stephanie had been an only child and had been engaged to be married, and she made sure Pat knew that she had robbed her family of their future. But Pat already knew, and her six-month conviction for drunken driving was never going to be enough to alleviate her conscience.

Sam finally left Ricky in early 1993 to work on a cruise ship, and the lad was broken-hearted. He went into business with his dad repairing the cars on Frank's lot and the two of them muddled through together while Pat was inside.

When she was released after three months, Frank decided to take her away from it all for a while and so they joined Grant, Phil, Kathy and Sharon on a day trip to Calais to stock up on some cheap wine and good food. And while he was in France, Frank wanted to check out an address he had for Diane in Paris. But when he knocked on the door he got the surprise of his life – Diane was eight months' pregnant!

Frank displayed all the traits that had made Diane run from him in the first place. He demanded that she return to Walford with him, he insulted her flatmates with his xenophobic and racist jargon, and insisted that she was too young to have a baby. Pat mediated, pointing out that she hadn't been too young to travel Europe by herself, hadn't been too young to get pregnant and that he was the one in a foreign country. But Frank, stubborn as ever, would not concede that he was wrong and stormed out.

Diane rushed to the ferry to try and make peace with her dad, but it was too late. Through hand signals they agreed to stay in touch and a month later Frank learnt that he was a granddad. (Pat too is a grandparent, and sees as much of Cindy and Simon's son Steven as Ian will allow.)

Frank's youngest daughter, Janine, was also about to cause the Butchers more grief. Clare had phoned to say she could take care of her no longer, and Pat and Frank welcomed her back to Albert Square with open arms. They even chucked Ricky out on to the streets (well, the campervan on the car lot) so that she could have her own room.

But she was still as troublesome as ever. Frank's authoritarian bullying didn't help matters either, still, Pat was around and keen to do a better job with Frank's kids than she'd done with her own. She offered Janine dresses, parties, anything she wanted. She treated her as much like an adult as she could, but Janine still acted like a spoilt brat.

She refused to go to school, feigning illness that no doctor could detect. On the days when she was forced to go to school she stocked up on junk food either from the kitchen cupboards or bought stuff from the café. It soon became clear that she was buying them for the kids at school.

But she wasn't trying to brag, or buy friends – she was being bullied. Unfortunately, like the little boy who cried wolf, everyone thought her protestations were just more of her trademark behaviour. And so she suffered the playground bullies in silence.

The problems snowballed for the Butchers when the money worries wouldn't go away. The violent sabotage campaign from a rival cab firm (the thugs even assaulted Pat) forced Frank to shut F&P cabs down. They moved from the flat at number 43 next door to the house at 41 where there was room for Ricky (and Diane and her son if she ever wanted to return), before Frank had a confirmed buyer for the flat. The burden of two mortgages was too much, and Pat took a cleaning job at the Vic, the pub where she had once been the landlady – she wasn't going to let Frank's pride lead them to bankruptcy.

Frank was forced to accept a ridiculously low offer from Phil for the flat in early 1994, but this tribe has survived greater hardships than cash-flow problems, and with Pat at the helm, they'll do their East End damnedest to pull through. And the arrival in January 1994 of Pat's eldest, David (whom she hadn't seen since he was sixteen) makes this brood bigger – and more troublesome – than ever.

Pat has changed so much since her arrival in the Square. She still has canny advice for women when it comes to men, but she never needs any herself. Frank's her man and she never looks at another bloke. The truth is, after years of sleeping around, and years of abuse from Brian Wicks, Pat had given up on finding stability and a loving family. Consequently she loves Frank, his kids and his faults, more than anything. She's thankful that he came back into her life, and she knows she's lucky. She could so easily have ended up running a brothel instead of a B&B.

SANJAY AND GITA KAPOOR

Asian families haven't had a happy time in Albert Square in the past. Naima and Saeed Jeffrey, the Bangladeshis who ran the convenience store in Bridge Street, hit misery when their marriage crumbled. She refused to have sex with him, and so he turned to making dirty phone calls and visiting prostitutes.

When Saeed returned to Bangladesh, Naima was courted by 'suitable cousins', and to her amazement fell for Farrukh and she too returned to Bangladesh in order to marry him.

Their replacements in First Til Last were the Karims, whose marriage was also shaken when Sufia discovered Ashraf had been having an affair for years.

And it seems that the Kapoors too have had their fair share of marital slings and arrows. The couple met when they were at college together and fell in love, much to the disappointment of Gita's family.

Everyone thought Gita could do better for herself, but Sanjay was determined to prove them wrong. He built up a successful business importing clothing from abroad, but things went wrong when Sanjay let Richard Cole get his tricky fingers on the outfit. Gita was convinced that Richard's mysterious meddling led to the downfall of Sanjay's business. Sanjay, however, blamed the recession and has strangely always defended Tricky Dicky against Gita's accusations.

Gita's mistrust of Richard is complicated; he believes it's because she fancies him! However it is true that in a moment of despair (before she moved to the Square), she asked Richard to hold her. He refused and left her crying.

The collapse of Sanjay's thriving empire gave Gita's

matriarchal family the chance they'd longed for to prove their theory that he was good for nothing. He started gambling and boozing, and even though she was pregnant with their first child, Gita didn't need much persuading to leave him.

Sanjay was determined to win her back and provide for his new family. He resolved to quit the gambling and start again. He asked his old pal Richard, who was now the market inspector in Walford, to help him out. Dicky gave Sanjay Rachel Kominsky's prize pitch in Bridge Street, and so Sanj started flogging designer threads again, but in a far more low-key operation than before. While he saved up for the deposit for a flat he stayed rent-free with Richard.

When Gita learnt that Sanjay was really making a go of things, she tracked him down to the Square. She was thrilled to see him again, but worried and annoyed that yet again he'd fallen into line behind Richard Cole. The couple went from vicious crockery-throwing fights one minute to tender embraces the next – it was clear that these two were going to bring much passion and intrigue with them to their new home.

Sanjay promised his wife that they would have a place of their own before the baby was born, but he found himself seduced by old temptations and got involved in a poker game in the Vic. He lost his £800 deposit for a flat to Nigel Bates on a foolish bluff.

Gita was heartbroken. Yet again he had let her down and if she hadn't been nine months' pregnant and in desperate need of her husband, she would have left him once more. But he promised to make it up to her, and as he was obviously still in love with her, she gave him another chance.

So Sanjay secretly borrowed money from Richard for a deposit on one of the flats at number 43 Albert Square, and after the birth of their daughter Sharmilla the couple moved into their new home.

Gita's joy at becoming a mum and seeing Sanjay straighten himself out was short-lived as tragedy was just around the corner. Her elderly mother died unexpectedly, causing much grief for her and her sisters Meena and Indira.

Meena started to spend a lot of time in Walford comforting her sister and antagonising her brother-in-law. Sparks flew when they were in a room – he thought she was a snob, and she thought he was a slob. Meena couldn't believe that Sanjay would rather spend time in the pub or at the dog track than comfort his wife. The truth is Sanjay would have done anything for his wife if Meena hadn't been hanging around and interfering.

A kind of respect existed between Meena and Sanjay and it was conceivable to see that perhaps he had married the wrong sister! After all, there's a fine line between love and hate. So when Sanjay returned home to find Meena weeping at the loss of her mother, he was willing to drop his guard and comfort her.

Now that Meena knew the softer side of Sanjay she could see the attraction, and the two started seeing each other in secret. Gita was suspicious of her shifty stall-holder and had a hunch he was cheating on her, so when he started giving Michelle Fowler driving lessons she accused him of having an affair with Michelle!

But Sanjay was being more deceitful than Gita could ever imagine, and in January 1994 she returned home to find her husband in bed with her sister.

Sanjay's betrayal underlines how secretive he can be. If there's a canny way of making money at the dog track, or there's a new supplier for counterfeit gear, Sanjay's bound to know. And one day he will make Gita wish she'd taken her family's advice and married a more suitable man.

THE JACKSONS

It was a tough act to follow, but Carol Jackson did her best to fill Dot's shoes in the launderette. Well, for someone who's used to doing her dirty washing in public, it came naturally.

Carol first appeared in *EastEnders* in November 1993, worrying and complaining about her wayward daughter Bianca, who had got to 'that age'. Carol worried that the sixteen-year-old would get pregnant like she had (Carol was fifteen when she found she was carrying Bianca) and she wanted to make sure Bianca broke the mould.

Carol is pure East End, born and raised on the poverty line that runs through the heart of Walford. She was determined to prove to her peers that she could cope with raising her baby – even if she was only a teenager.

She had to be tough. Every man she was ever involved with was bad news, and it wasn't long before her second child was on the way. But Carol was no tart; she was just looking for affection. And in her teenage naivety she muddled sex and love.

When her son Robbie was six, Carol discovered she was pregnant yet again, but even though Sonia was her third child by a third man, she still wasn't going to lie down and take life's blows.

Carol was a fighter and she always made sure that whenever she could scrape together a few extra pennies for her kids, she would work all the hours God sent. She was never going to let anyone tell her – or anyone else in her family – that she was a loser.

In 1988, she met Alan Jackson, a good-natured black man who was five years younger than her and said he loved her. Only this time he really did love her, and he meant it when he said he would take care of her and her kids.

Alan is a decent bloke who doesn't ask for much, but will give you anything he has – as long as he's got enough left over for a pint and a bet.

Although Alan and Carol never actually got round to tying the knot, they still lived together as man and wife in a flat in Walford Towers and in 1989 they had a son together, Billy, who is just about the cutest kid Walford's ever seen.

Things started going wrong for this unusual family when Alan lost his job at one of the East End's huge car plants as the recession kicked in. The lost wages meant Carol had to work even harder to provide for her children, which often led to her temper getting out of control. And the fact that she wasn't around to dish out the discipline meant Bianca and Robbie were given a chance to go off the rails.

Robbie started playing hookey from school and Bianca entered the world of sex and booze much earlier than her parents would have liked. Robbie has turned out to be the local delinquent. He's very streetwise and could have a good future as a crook – or a bent copper.

As Carol toiled in the Bridge Street launderette, she fretted about her offspring. When she found out that a dress Bianca had bought off Sanjay cost £35, and not a tenner as she'd said, Carol was ready for a fight. She doesn't even smoke because she can't afford it, and here was her daughter blowing a week's wages on a dress that was far too grand for anything in Walford.

Sparks fly between this feisty mother and daughter because they are too much alike. Carol is guilty of accusing her daughter of her own sins, but Bianca would rather go on the Pill than have a baby. Nevertheless, her temperament is as fiery as her red hair, and Bianca will always give her mum as good as she gets.

Thankfully Sonia doesn't give her mum half as many problems. She's settled into the East Enders' way of life fairly smoothly and is in the same class as Martin Fowler at Walford Primary School.

Billy is unlikely to cause too much trouble either – as long as his adoring daddy is around to play with him.

The family moved from the estate to Albert Square in early 1994, and their arrival raised a few eyebrows. Locals are quick to gossip about newcomers, and let's face it, there's plenty to be said about the Jacksons. But their unlawfully wedded state, the fact that Alan is obviously not Bianca, Robbie and Sonia's real dad, and their mixed-race relationship doesn't matter to the Jacksons. If the windbags want to gossip, let them: the Jacksons have thick enough East End skin to endure pretty much anything. And if Robbie doesn't con too many of the neighbours, they look set to stay put in Albert Square for a while.

LIFE IN ALBERT SQUARE

ALBERT SQUARE AND WALFORD

The East End of London has always been like a little village, almost unaware that one of the world's greatest cities was growing up around it.

Traditionally an area where hard work was the only way to escape poverty, East Enders have never been afraid of toiling from dawn to dusk. High unemployment meant everyone knew there was a queue of willing workers lined up to take their place if they started slacking. Consequently, East Enders are a hardy lot, bred to endure great hardships.

In Victorian times, the main employer was the docks down on the Thames. The docks also brought in new ideas, goods and peoples from all over the world. Whether it was the Irish escaping the potato blight, or Jews fleeing massacre or Bengalis looking for a new life, immigrants have always found a home in the East End.

The industrial revolution and the building boom of Victorian times exerted a major influence in Walford. Firstly, the area was established as a manufacturing centre for material and clothes, not to mention a trading mecca for fresh produce, and of course two-up two-down houses like those in Albert Square sprang up everywhere.

The quiet little streets and squares made it an ideal place to bring up families. The small houses and lack of money to move on meant that several generations lived together in very cramped conditions, making a sense of 'family' strong in the minds of East Enders.

Albert Square and its environs were built round about the 1880s. Some of the properties are council owned, like the Fowlers' at number 45, and some are privately owned, like next door at number 43.

There has been a street market in the area since people can remember. The only time it ceased trading was during World War II, when many of the stall-holders were sent to fight for their country.

The Blitz bombings had a crippling effect on Walford; not only were huge areas (like where the Estate is now) razed to the ground, but many people were killed and lives and livelihoods destroyed. The Queen Victoria pub was very nearly obliterated by a doodlebug which struck the house behind (number 47).

The black market in rationed goods thrived in the East End. The close-knit family ties meant no one would blab and the docks provided a steady supply of illicit goods. But an underbelly of crime and protection rackets had been commonplace in the area for generations. However, it was only after the war that the East End really got its reputation as gangland central.

Even though the Kray twins (notorious gangsters Ronnie and Reggie who maintained a vicious protection racket) were jailed in the 1960s, major crime syndicates still exist in the area. The governors of Walford are the Firm, who proved when they murdered Den Watts in 1989 that they will kill to get what they want.

But far greater employers than crime these days are the huge car plants and factories in metropolitan Essex, and of course the clothing industry still thrives with sweat shops behind several locked doors along the high streets of East End boroughs.

The Government initiative to renovate the whole Docklands area had an incredible impact on East End life in the 1980s. Suddenly the values that had stood the area in good stead for generations were thrown out the window by outsiders with clipboards, hard hats and balance sheet mentalities.

Although Albert Square isn't in the shadow of developments like Canary Wharf, the 1980s boom still had an effect on the community. The yuppies who worked in the new office towers started to move into the area, buying up houses as investments and tarting them up before moving on.

The East End is constantly changing, but throughout the flux of immigration, industrial decay and the ever-present threat of crime, East End values of family remain constant. Like no other place in London, Walford has retained its sense of community, almost as if it was in a time warp.

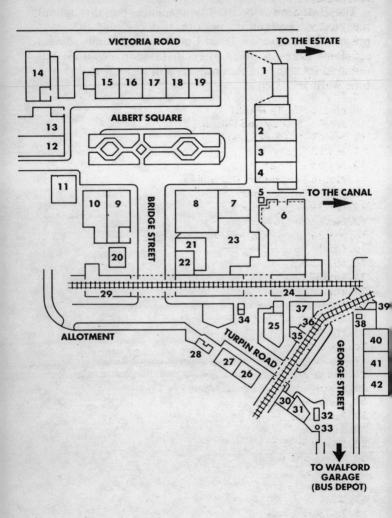

Map of Albert Square and surrounding area

1. Frank's car lot
2. No.5 Squat
3. No.3 Kathy/Ian's
4. No.1 Dr. Legg's
5. Phone box
6. Playground
7. No.47 (Mark's)
8. The Vic
9. No.45 (The Fowler's)
10. No.43 (Sanjay and Gita's)
11. No.41 (The Butcher's)
12. No.18 Empty
13. No.20 The B&B
14. No.55 Victoria Rd. (Michelle's)
15. No.31 Empty squat
16. No.29 Empty squat
17. No.27 The Tavernier's
18. No.25 Council house (formerly Dot's)
19. No.23 Vacant (Reg Cox's)
20. The Cafe
21. First til Last
22. The Laundrette
23. Community centre
24. The Arches (Phil's repair shop)
25. The Dagmar
26. Video shop
27. No.13 Turpin Rd: Betting shop (Richard Cole's)
28. The Green Lantern Takeaway
29. Pizza Parlour (Formerly 'Strokes')
30. Metal workshop
31. Post office
32. Bus stop
33. Post box
34. Telephone boxes
35. Pet shop
36. Furniture store
37. Yard
38. Telephone box
39. Gent's public toilets
40. No.87 George St.
41. No.89 George St.
42. No.91 George St.

ALBERT SQUARE BUILDING BY BUILDING

1. FRANK'S CAR LOT
Frank started using the site as a second-hand car yard in March 1989. The plot had formerly been a discount tyre centre. The portakabin on the site also doubled as the radio base for F&P Cabs.

2. NUMBER FIVE
A formerly council-owned property which had been vacant and derelict for years. It was opened up as a squat in 1993 by Mandy and Aidan, but they were evicted at Christmas that year by Richard Cole who had bought the building hoping to make money on the deal. However, the property needed substantial renovation.

3. NUMBER THREE
Bought by Tony Carpenter in the mid-1980s as an invest-ment. He converted the three-storey house into flats, keeping the basement for himself and selling the top flat to Colin Russell. The ground level flat was later taken by Carmel Roberts.

After Colin moved to Bristol, Rod and Donna squatted in his flat, which is now owned by Ian Beale. His mum, Kathy, owns the basement flat. This is a well-maintained building in a good state of repair.

4. NUMBER ONE
In the basement is Dr Legg's surgery, and on the upper levels are flats, one of which was rented to Ethel Skinner before she moved in with Dot, and the other to Lofty Holloway. After Ethel, the flat was taken over by Pat Wicks before she moved into the Vic. Michelle and Vicki

moved into the top flat while Michelle was married to Lofty.

Dr Legg now lives in the house having given up his other property in Islington.

5. PHONE BOX

6. CHILDREN'S PLAY AREA
Run by the London Borough of Walford, this rundown playground is one of the few places for kids in the neighbourhood. It was built on waste ground created by a bombshell during the war.

7. NUMBER FORTY-SEVEN
This 1960s-built maisonette replaced the terraced house lost during the Blitz. The ground floor is owned and occupied by Alan McIntyre, who rents the first floor (47a) to Mark Fowler and Nigel Bates. Mark previously shared the flat with Steve Elliot. Former tenants include Sue and Ali Osman.

8. THE QUEEN VICTORIA PUBLIC HOUSE
Renovated in 1992 following a fire started by present landlord Grant Mitchell. His wife Sharon grew up in the flat above the pub, while her parents Den and Angie Watts served the punters in the bar. When Den left, Pat and Frank Butcher became the landlords, followed by Eddie Royle. Sharon became the licensee following Eddie's murder.

9. NUMBER FORTY-FIVE
The council have rented this house to the Beale family for generations. Pauline, Pete, Kenny, Mark and Michelle have all grown up in this house. Lou died here (in the front room) in 1988, and Pauline became the official council tenant. It is also home to Martin and Arthur. Wicksy, Ian, Aidan and Naima have all been lodgers in the past.

The Fowlers got the money to redecorate in 1988, but Pauline chose exactly the same wallpaper as had been there before! They also bought a new carpet with a rich red and brown crystal pattern which hides stains. The furniture harks back to the days of Lou, but Pete did fit a kitchen for his sis a few years ago.

There is only one loo in the house, the other one being outside in the yard, although this is now used as a shed.

10. NUMBER FORTY-THREE

This house was bought by bank clerk Debbie Wilkins in 1984, and she lived here with her long-term boyfriend, male nurse Andy O'Brien. Debs got a special mortgage rate from her employers and so could afford to renovate the building. She painted the outside baby blue and installed a fitted kitchen with pine panelling.

Following Andy's death and Debs' marriage to DS Rich, she sold the house to James Willmott-Brown who in turn sold to local property owner Alan McIntyre, who converted the place into flats.

43a (downstairs) was bought by Den Watts in 1988, and Sharon, Michelle and Vicki lived there until 1990 when Sharon sold to Grant Mitchell. 43b was bought by Grant's brother Phil, who purchased the property from Julie Cooper.

The brothers tried to reopen the partition between the flats before selling up to buy into the Vic. Frank bought 43a in 1990 and redecorated with flowery wallpaper, and he lived there with Pat until November 1993 when Ricky and Janine moved back in, forcing him to buy a bigger property – number 41 next door.

In January 1994, Frank sold the flat to Phil Mitchell for £20,000 who now lives there alone.

Number 43b has been redecorated in simple blues and creams, and is currently occupied by Sanjay and Gita Kapoor.

11. NUMBER FORTY-ONE

The new family home for the Butchers. Pat, Frank, Ricky, Janine and David Wicks all live here – and there's room enough for Diane if she ever wants to return.

12. NUMBER EIGHTEEN
Another previous residence of the Butcher family. They lived here when they owned the B&B next door, to which there used to be a connecting door.

13. NUMBER TWENTY
The Bed and Breakfast. Originally owned by the infamous Doris who was a bit of a man eater and could give a male guest more than he bargained for! It was subsequently owned and run by Pat and Frank who left the building in 1992.

14. FIFTY-FIVE VICTORIA ROAD
Owned by Rachel Kominsky who now lives in Leeds. She rents the property to Michelle Fowler and Shelley Lewis. Previously the property of the Karims.

15. NUMBER THIRTY-ONE
Has been derelict and empty for many years.

16. NUMBER TWENTY-NINE
Another council-owned property that has been left vacant for years.

17. NUMBER TWENTY-SEVEN
Owned by Celestine and Etta Tavernier who now live in East Anglia, but Celestine's dad Jules still lives here.

18. NUMBER TWENTY-FIVE
A council-owned property, once let to Tom Clements who swapped residences with Dot Cotton in 1987 to live next door in a bedsit. Dot lived there with Ethel for a while, and has since had a succession of lodgers: Pat, Nigel, Donna (who died in the front room), and Rod.

Following Dot's departure from the Square in 1993, the house was empty for a while, before the council installed the Jacksons, who inherited Dot's unusual taste in decor – notably her purple and green kitchen.

19. NUMBER TWENTY-THREE

Reg Cox died in the bedsit on the first floor which was later rented to single mum Mary Smith. The bedsit was redecorated by the council after Mary's baby Annie started a fire when she was left alone. Sue and Ali Osman lived in the ground floor bedsit until the death of their son Hassan, when the memories became too painful and they moved to number 47a. Dot lived there after them until she moved next door in 1987.

20. THE CAFE

Once called Al's Café after its owner Ali Osman, this was also the base for his cab company Ozcabs. In an attempt to attract more trade (and keep the health inspectors at bay), they tarted the place up in 1986 painting the woodwork lime green. Despite various changes in ownership (Ian took over from Ali, and later sold to Kath, Pauline and Frank), the decor remained the same until 1992 when Kathy bought Pauline out and redecorated to convert the café into a bistro. Kathy still served traditional English breakfasts during the day, but opened up as a classy French bistro at night. She installed a pink neon sign in the window which read 'Kathy's', and set about moving the Bridge St Café upmarket.

Unfortunately, Walford wasn't ready for sophistication, and Kath closed the Bistro, but stayed open as a typical East End café in the daytime.

21. FIRST TIL LAST

A convenience store and off-licence owned by Mrs Andreas. The previous owners were the Karims, who bought the business from Ashraf's second cousins, the Jeffreys. Saeed and Naima Jeffrey ran the family business together until their marriage disintegrated, when Naima carried on alone until she remarried.

As well as the various owners over the years, First Til Last has been an employer for Debs, Donna, Tina, Aidan and Mandy.

22. THE BRIDGE STREET LAUNDERETTE
Owned by Mr Opidopoulous and run by Pauline Fowler and Carol Jackson who work alternate shifts. Carol took over Dot's shifts in November 1993.

23. DEMOLITION SITE
Formerly the site of the community centre which was used for jumble sales, nativity plays, Brownie meetings – as well as the occasional dubious event (remember Darren's screening of porn videos?) – the Walford community centre is a much used local resource. It is also the local polling station on Election Day. Both Mo and Tom have been caretakers here in their time.

24. THE ARCHES
Underneath the railway bridge there are several small businesses operating out of what the locals call 'the Arches'. One such business is Phil Mitchell's crash-repair garage which is situated here.

25. THE MEAL MACHINE
This former pub was the local hangout for prostitutes and addicts before James Willmott-Brown renovated it in 1987 and reopened it as the Dagmar. It was razed in an arson attack in 1988 and the burnt-out shell became home for tramp Jackie Stone and his friends. Ian Beale leased the reconditioned premises in 1991 as a base for his catering business, the Meal Machine. He moved out of his offices in 1993 to work from home and the property is now vacant.

26. VIDEO SHOP
The local video hire shop used to be Julie's hair salon, owned by Julie Cooper. Before that it had been the Turpin Road Fish Bar.

27. TURF ACCOUNTANT
The local betting shop. Richard Cole lives in the flat upstairs at 13a Turpin Road.

28. THE GREEN LANTERN
The local Chinese take-away.

29. PIZZA PARLOUR
This was originally Harry's Wine Bar before the Firm bought it and reopened it as Strokes. It later became a pizza parlour but is now vacant.

30. METAL WORKSHOP

31. POST OFFICE
Another focus of the Walford gossip machine!

32. BUS STOP

33. POST BOX

34. TELEPHONE BOXES

35. PET SHOP

36. FURNITURE STORE

37. YARD

38. TELEPHONE BOX

39. GENTS PUBLIC TOILETS

40. EIGHTY-SEVEN GEORGE STREET
The George Street section of Walford was an addition to the Albert Square set in 1993, although it wasn't seen on screen until January 1994.

41. EIGHTY-NINE GEORGE STREET
This row of Victorian terraced houses was built at the same time as Albert Square, and like the Square, they are occupied by private residents.

42. NINETY-ONE GEORGE STREET

ADULTERY

It's a wonder that a solicitor hasn't opened up shop in Bridge Street because the marital slings and arrows of the folk in Albert Square could keep a divorce lawyer in business for life! And the gossips have been busy too. Walford's clandestine liaisons have made sure that someone's net curtains have always been twitching.

People who were once thought of as heroes became villains when they fell foul of temptation. The strong were seen to crumble as the deception destroyed them, and the meek suddenly seemed macho as they took a chance on happiness.

But the smiles inevitably turned to tears, because adulterers in Albert Square have never got away with it . . .

DEN WATTS AND JAN HAMMOND
1980–87

Angie always knew that her husband had another woman, and even though he knew she knew, he still had the decency to pretend it was the brewery on the other end of the phone whenever Angie entered the room.

The grey BT-issue phone in the hall of the Queen Victoria became a symbol for Jan, her only avenue to infiltrate Angie's territory. Jan was never allowed to visit the Square, so Den was often seen slipping furtively into his Rover for yet another rendezvous.

They were an odd couple. She was a cultured woman with a successful career in personnel, and he was a scally cut from rough cloth who had never gone to the theatre, let alone read a book. They had nothing in common – but it worked.

For years Jan was happy to remain a figure in the distance. She didn't want to have to do Den's washing, or consult him before accepting a job offer. She was too independent to need a husband, but she enjoyed the companionship, and the sex, and was happy with the status quo.

Den was always slightly in awe of his mistress and her sophisticated ways – she was the sort of lady East End lads didn't dare dream about. And she was convenient. Jan didn't demand too many hours, didn't ask him to leave his wife, or want any children. In fact, if he was careful Den knew he could cheat on her too.

But that changed in February 1986 when Jan's father died. She relied on Den for emotional support and she desperately needed to fall apart in his arms and cry on his shoulder. And so in the middle of a drag show at the Queen Vic, Jan walked into the bar. The goalposts were changed – and now Angie would have to face her rival, and Den would have to make a decision.

He chose Jan. He moved into her house while lying (yet again) to Angie that he had rented a bedsit. But Jan found it difficult having Den permanently in her space, and they started to argue. When Den returned to the Vic after a row with his mistress, he found his wife comatose after an overdose and vowed to stick with Angie. But when things turned sour Angie told him she was dying, and yet again he decided to stick by his wife.

Den took her on a second honeymoon to Venice where he bumped into Jan, on holiday visiting her Italian boyfriend Dario. It was clear there was still a strong attraction between the publican and his former mistress. So when Den discovered Angie was lying about her 'terminal illness', it wasn't long before he went running back to Jan.

While he plotted his divorce from Angie, Den paved the way for Jan to join him in the Vic. But Jan was a flop behind the bar, and she couldn't swap her designer threads for the knock-off version on the market stalls. And despite all her personnel skills she couldn't handle the staff at the pub. She tried to fire Pat and succeeded in firing Pauline who was doing the cleaning at the time.

It was also Jan's first chance to see Den as he really was. And the creature in his natural habitat was more of a rat than Jan had ever imagined. He flagrantly broke the law, fiddled the books and flirted with his customers. And he still let Angie get under his skin.

Jan realised that their relationship had been much stronger when it was conducted on the phone, and she noted that if she didn't leave Den – and his downmarket lifestyle – now, she'd be stuck with him for life.

She returned to the Vic one last time to collect her things at the same time as Angie. And the two women felt real glee at the irony of the wife and the mistress walking out on Walford's notorious womaniser at the same time. Even Den managed a smile.

ANGIE WATTS AND TONY CARPENTER
APRIL–MAY 1985

Tony was the gentle giant of Albert Square in the early days. He would listen and offer little advice, just a warm hug and a friendly smile. As the local handyman he was often in the Vic fixing a burst pipe or giving a quote for building a partition.

He was separated from his wife Hannah with whom he had two children, Kelvin and Cassie. Hannah and Cassie lived with Hannah's new man Neville in another part of London, while Tony tried to bring up Kelvin at number 3. Although he got on well with Angie and had been lonely for a while, he never imagined that he might have an affair with her.

But she had just found out that her husband Den had been on holiday with his mistress, Jan, and not alone as he had said. And so Angie devised a plot to get even with Den, to start playing the games with him that he had played with her for years. Angie resolved that she would have a revenge affair – just as soon as she found a man.

Her victim was poor old Tony, and unfortunately he didn't realise he was just a pawn in another Den/Angie mind game. He became really fond of her – he even gave her a gold bracelet to show her his affection. But when Den returned from Spain and saw that Angie hadn't missed him as expected, he was prompted to say he would stop his affair if she would stop hers. Angie was only too happy to oblige.

While the warring Wattses tried again for the umpteenth time, Tony was left feeling used and confused. He tried to make his feelings known to Angie, but when he saw Sharon wearing the bracelet, he resigned himself to the fact that it was a lost cause.

DEN WATTS AND MICHELLE FOWLER
AUGUST 1985

The fact that Michelle was his daughter's best mate didn't seem to bother Dennis Watts. She came to him in a time of need for advice, and he ended up claiming her virginity as payment for services rendered. And dirty rat that he was, Den typically avoided accusations that he had slept with a minor as the deed happened just after Michelle's sixteenth birthday.

No one knew about their night of passion; the only clue was when they avoided each other in the market, breathing a sigh of relief when the other had passed. After Michelle had come clean to her folks that she was pregnant she arranged to meet Den by the canal, away from the intrusive gossips of Albert Square. She told the reluctant father that she wasn't going to have an abortion and that she didn't blame him. 'It could have been anyone,' she informed him. 'If it wasn't you it would have been somebody else. But it wasn't sordid. After sixteen years it was an important event, but I never thought it would happen on a plastic bench in a saloon bar under a picture of Queen Victoria.'

Den remained silent, and vowed to stay that way forever. But these ill-fated lovers couldn't deny their confused feelings for each other. Odd glances would be exchanged, tenners cautiously handed over and irrational things said within earshot of prying ears, and eventually Pauline guessed.

Apart from telling Sharon and Arthur, Michelle managed to keep her secret for eight years – a record for Albert Square!

DANNY WHITING AND MICHELLE FOWLER
JULY 1989–FEBRUARY 1990

Michelle had a habit of falling for older men because most of the guys her age were comparatively juvenile. She met Danny when he came to fix the surgery computer at Dr Legg's where she was working as a receptionist.

There was an instant attraction, and for a month or so Michelle truly thought that she had found a replacement for Den in her affections. But when she tried to ring him at work, and one of his colleagues referred to her as his wife, Michelle realised that once again her love life had been jinxed.

But even though she knew Danny was married – and had three kids – she couldn't stop seeing him and believed him when he said he wanted to leave his wife. So when he turned up on her doorstep with suitcase in hand, she justifiably thought he had left his wife Mandy. But the truth was that she'd thrown him out.

They celebrated Christmas together, but their toast to a happy future hit a snag when Danny gave Michelle his wife's Christmas card by mistake.

Like most adulterers, Danny'd lied to both his wife and his lover. But it was only when Mandy refused to take him back that he persuaded Michelle that she and Vicki should relocate with him to Newcastle.

The bags were packed, the car was waiting, but at the last second Michelle backed out. She knew that he wasn't a father for her daughter or a man she could really trust. But more than that, she knew she belonged in Albert Square.

ASHRAF KARIM AND STELLA 1968–90

Ashraf and his family took over the First Til Last shop in Bridge Street (which had previously been owned by Ashraf's second cousin Naima Jeffrey) in 1988 after selling their other shop in Walford High Street. At first it seemed he was a loving and faithful husband to his wife Sufia, but in November it became clear that Sufia's suspicions had been well founded.

Ashraf had met Stella in 1968 when he'd visited Britain as a student. He fell in love with hippy Stella but had to return to Bangladesh because he was already engaged to Sufia.

After their wedding, Ashraf and Sufia emigrated to Britain in 1973 and had two children, Shireen and Sohail. Ashraf was a born Lothario, and as well as reviving his relationship with Stella, he also saw many other mistresses.

Sufia was not blind to his betrayals and in January 1990 she decided she had finally had enough and packed her bags. Ashraf caught her leaving but managed to persuade her that everything was over with his mistress. But not because he had ended it out of decency, but because Stella had become weary of playing second fiddle and had decided to make the break.

No more was seen of Stella until the uncle of Shireen's fiancé spotted Ashraf with her in a restaurant. Shamed at the thought of marrying into a family of adulterers, the uncle put a stop to the wedding and Ashraf and his family were forced to move to Bristol to distance themselves from the affair.

CINDY BEALE AND SIMON WICKS
AUGUST 1990–MARCH 1992

Ever since Wicksy spotted Cindy working on her mum's hat stall in Turpin Road, there was little doubt that the two of them would end up in bed together. But when Cindy saw Simon with another girl she decided to make him jealous. And what better way of turning a red-blooded man green with envy than by going for his best mate?

The fact that Simon and Ian may or may not have been half-brothers had been put behind them, and the two likely lads had become firm friends. Ian, however, was naive and inexperienced compared with Cindy and Simon and had no idea that Cindy was only faking it.

Although Simon was undeniably attracted to Cindy, he knew better than to sleep with his best mate's girl. His resolution to deny his feelings for her increased when Ian proposed in February 1989.

But in May that year after a couple of after-hours drinks in the Queen Vic, Cindy and Wicksy made love. And like Michelle before her, one night in the saloon bar was all it took for Cindy and two months later she announced she was pregnant.

Ian was overjoyed as he had no idea the baby wasn't his, and they married shortly before Steven's premature birth on Boxing Day 1989. But once Wicksy had seen and held his son, it wasn't long before he begged Cindy to run away with him. Cindy was forced to tell Ian that Steven wasn't his, and the illicit lovers ran away with their son to Devon.

They stayed together for a while, but when Ian tracked his wife down in October 1992 to sign an insurance document, Wicksy had already left her. Ian was still in love with her and after much persuading, she returned to the Square.

They may share the same surname, but Sharon and Phil are not man and wife. She is married to his brother, and if quick-tempered Grant ever found out about their affair, he'd kill them.

Sharon and Grant had been married less than a year when she revealed to him that she did not want to have his baby. Grant took this as his licence to behave despicably, and started staying out all hours drinking with his mates. Phil, who lived with his brother and his wife above the Vic, could see how Grant's behaviour was affecting Sharon.

Phil had always had to apologise for his little brother, but he offered Sharon far more than excuses. He was the one she turned to for support and reassurance when all Grant could do was put her down. Phil's willingness to offer this attention masked his feelings of love for Sharon, and soon she felt the same way.

They tried to deny the inevitable for unbearably long months, because no matter how they felt about each other, they both still cared for Grant.

But when Grant was very late home from a drinking session, Sharon and Phil stole their moment and made passionate love. A few hours later, Grant staggered home so drunk that he couldn't realise what had happened. Phil told Sharon that if she went to bed with Grant that night there would never be a chance for the two of them again.

And although she went to bed with her drunk husband, she could not hide her feelings. Even thick-skinned Grant noticed her odd behaviour and asked her outright if there was anybody else. Sharon was so tempted to say yes, for the nightmare to be over and for her and Phil to start again. But out of duty she lied and said no.

Grant never quite believed her, and his temper still had the inflammable tendencies of petrol. So when a copper came round to question him about reported domestic violence, Grant belted him one. He was arrested for assaulting a police officer and held on remand.

Sharon and Phil seized the day and lived together while Grant was inside. The punters in the Vic noticed a change in Sharon, but none of them suspected she was sleeping with her husband's brother.

Neither of them could bring themselves to tell Grant while he was in prison, and they often argued over who should do the dirty deed. They argued for so long that Grant was released before either of them had plucked up the courage. Remarkably, it seemed that prison had changed Grant for the better.

Sharon gave her 'new' husband a second try but Phil couldn't bear to watch. The pain at seeing her with someone else forced him to move out of the Vic, but love was just around the corner for him too – with Kathy Beale.

ARTHUR FOWLER AND CHRISTINE HEWITT
DECEMBER 1992– SEPTEMBER 1993

Pauline and Arthur Fowler had one of the most successful marriages Walford has ever known. For 28 years they supported each other through tougher times than most folk could even imagine, and their marriage seemed all the stronger for it.

So when Arthur started gardening for bored suburban housewife Mrs Hewitt in the summer of 1992, there seemed little chance that her girlish flirtations would lead Arthur astray.

Christine's husband Greg had left her for a younger woman some months before, and the rejection made her want to prove to herself that she was still attractive to men.

In an attempt to stay close to Arthur, the man she'd obviously set her heart on, Christine begged Arthur to give her useless son Jonathan a job.

But Jonathan's inability to drag himself out of bed put

77

paid to that, and Christine had to come up with ever more contrived reasons for visiting the Square. Soon Arthur twigged what was on her mind, and when Pauline went to New Zealand for three months in the autumn of 1992, many thought her absence would provide Arthur with the opportunity to do more than tend Mrs H's flower beds!

When Jules Tavernier caught Christine planting a kiss on Arthur on video, many Walfordians thought the fellow had already done the dirty on his trusting wife.

But the truth was that Arthur had calmly turned down her advances. Even so, when the Square spotted that Christine had stayed overnight at number 45 (albeit on the sofa and only because Arthur had been too drunk to be responsible for Martin and Vicki), Arthur was hard pressed to convince anyone that his relationship with Mrs H was still platonic.

On her return from Down Under, even Pauline sensed there was something going on and she confronted Arthur with her suspicions.

What Pauline didn't know, however, was that her behaviour after her trip abroad would be what would finally drive her husband to another woman's bed. Pauline had been so enamoured of Kenny's swimming pool and his idyllic lifestyle that all she could do was put Walford – and Arthur – down.

She became an unbearable nag without a good word to say about anything. She tried to convince Arthur that they should emigrate to New Zealand, but Arthur wouldn't be budged. Pauline became so irritating to be around that Mrs Hewitt's house became a safe haven from the constant ear bashing, and Arthur started to retreat there more and more.

It wasn't until Christmas Eve 1992, though, that Arthur and Christine finally made love after she begged him not to leave her alone at Christmas.

Afterwards, Arthur guiltily rushed home to play good daddy to Martin the next day, but there would be several times in the following months when Arthur would be noticeably absent at family events.

It was when he wasn't there when little Vicki was kidnapped that the guilt started to eat him up, and for months he became agitated and restless. Pauline, now mellowed and quite happy in Walford once again, wondered if maybe there was a money or health problem he wasn't telling her about – she didn't think for a moment that he was carrying on.

Christine's husband Greg came back to 'claim' his wife in 1993, but she stubbornly refused to get back together with him – making it clear that Arthur was the only man she wanted. She even took a job as the cook at Kathy's Bistro in Bridge Street so she could see more of him. It was only a matter of time before she presented her paramour with an ultimatum: either he told Pauline, or she would!

But Arthur was desperate to confess the affair to Pauline anyway as he could no longer live with the guilt. He hoped that a confession would lead to a reunion, and so, on 9 September 1993, he wrote his wife a note revealing his sins.

But he knew that Pauline would respect him even less if he didn't tell her to her face. As he brooded in his armchair thinking of what words to use, Pauline started clearing up and found his screwed-up note.

'Pauline, don't read that,' he said. 'I don't want you to find out that way.'

'Find out what?'

And after an unbearable pause, Arthur said simply: 'I've been having an affair.'

Pauline's reaction was one of disbelief: 'You?'

But once his betrayal had sunk in, she let loose an attack that Lou Beale would have been proud of. Out came the frying pan, the crockery, the teapot – everything she could find to throw at him became a vengeful weapon. And her anger didn't stop with the violence – her rage led her to throw him out, and with his tail between his legs, Arthur sloped across the Square to doss with Mark.

Arthur paid a high price for his dalliance. At first Pauline stopped him seeing Martin, and refused to even speak to him when they passed each other in the market. Arthur became so depressed that he left Albert Square in the hope that Martin would forget about him. Foolishly, he thought that would be easier for the little lad. But Martin missed his dad terribly, and when he told his big sister Michelle that he thought Daddy hated him and had gone away, Michelle made it her business to make sure Arthur returned to the Square.

A chance sighting by Frank of Arthur leaving a doss-house was all the lead Michelle needed to track her dad down and bring him back home.

But Pauline wouldn't let him back inside number 45. However, Arthur was willing to be patient and, as often happens, it was to be tragedy that finally brought them back together.

Pauline confessed that she couldn't have got through Pete's death and funeral without Arthur's gentle support. She realised that he was pretty pathetic without her, and she was better with him. And so on New Year's Eve, she invited him home on the understanding that they would have separate beds – anything more, they agreed, would come in time.

SANJAY KAPOOR AND MEENA MACKENZIE
OCTOBER 1993 JANUARY 1994

Sanjay had always fought like cat and dog with his haughty sister-in-law Meena. But like Tracy and Hepburn or Katharine and Petruchio, beneath their bickering was an undeniable attraction.

Following the death of her mother, Meena started to spend a lot of time in Albert Square so she could grieve with her younger sister Gita. But with her sister and her husband constantly point-scoring, it was the rows more than anything else that were making Gita miserable.

One day, Sanjay popped home to make a phone call and found Meena weeping in his living room. It was an instinctive reaction to offer comfort by hugging her. When they touched they could both feel that what was between them was more than comfort.

Secretly, they started to see each other. Gita would catch Sanjay making phone calls and changing the subject whenever she came in the room and she became suspicious that he was cheating on her.

When she noticed how much time he was spending with Michelle Fowler, Gita thought she had found his other woman. But it turned out that Sanjay was giving Michelle driving lessons. It wasn't until the following January that the identity of Sanjay's mistress was known, but when the truth surfaced it was the Square's most shocking revelation for years.

BADDIES

The East End is teaming with villains. The Kray twins may have been inside for years, but their ilk still patrol the area. The particular guardians of Walford are the Firm, and many of Albert Square's residents have links to this ruthless gang. The Mitchell brothers have done more than the odd dodgy deal in their time, and even Frank Butcher can tell you where the next lorry will casually drop its load.

The Firm's most notorious Albert Square associate was Den Watts, formerly publican of the Queen Victoria public house. Den would often launder money or hide wanted men for the Firm, who used Brad Williams as their go-between.

But although Den and the Mitchells are criminals, they are not evil; they don't hurt their own, and sometimes they even come across as heroes. Albert Square's real home-grown villain was Nick Cotton, a man whose only motivation in life was to make other people suffer. He was a first-class bully without a conscience.

But there are still some people who are even more loathed in Walford than Nick – the Filth. Talking to a policeman in Walford is a sin that encourages suspicion and alienation. No one calls for police help in the East End; natural justice is the preferred method of sorting baddies out, and many a slimeball has been the victim of an Albert Square lynch mob.

IAN BEALE

Ian changed from a mild-mannered barrow boy to an over-zealous megalomaniac virtually overnight. As a kid he had always been weedy, and it took all the strength he had to stand up to the machismo of his dad Pete when Ian announced he was going to catering college.

Even Ian had no idea that when he left college he would have more job offers than he could handle. Den wanted him to do the lunches in the Vic, Willmott-Brown wanted him to do the catering in the Dagmar, Mags wanted him as an assistant and Ali wanted him in the café.

All this flattery went to his head and he soon realised that he could play them all off against each other until he got the best deal.

When Ali needed money to keep the café afloat, Ian lent it to him. And when Ali couldn't repay, Ian seized control and it was the start of his catering empire.

He starting delivering meals to the Vic and set about finding premises to start his own catering company, Beales on Wheels. He became obsessed with money-making and seemed to derive pleasure from flaunting his new jeep in front of his poorer neighbours and family.

He decided that the burnt-out shell of the Dagmar was perfect for his new, more up-market company, The Meal Machine, and he decided to buy it. The only problem was that the former pub had tramps squatting in it. So Ian planted stolen computer equipment in the pub and tipped off the police using his mobile phone.

His lack of emotion and disregard for his loved ones' feelings was acutely displayed when his mum Kathy begged him not to buy the Dagmar – it was the building where she had been raped and it had terrible memories for her. But cruel Ian was having none of it and went ahead with his renovation.

Ian by now had a family of his own: Cindy, and her son Steven. But his obsession with the almighty Pound distanced them from each other, so that when she left him for Wicksy his only avenue for comfort was to try to make more money.

He became ruthless and vindictive, taking his pain out on his employees. At one point he lit a fire in a waste-paper bin and held his hand in the flames to see how much pain he could withstand. He became starved of affection and tried to force himself on Hattie. But he has never forgotten that she was the only person who always stood by him and he has a genuine soft spot for the girl.

Ian believes Albert Square is his manor and he's more than ready to stand up for his mum, or Cindy, or any other Beale. But even so he still cannot be trusted. Unless there's something in it for him, Ian Beale will screw you for every penny you have.

RICHARD COLE

Tricky Dicky should come with a health warning: Do Not Trust This Man. Richard Cole thinks he's a big fish in a small pond, but he's more like a playground bully than a man-eating shark. And anyway, he'd much rather eat women. Richard Cole truly believes he is a god-given gift to the female of the species.

He thinks he can have any woman he wants, but both Cindy and Shelley Lewis turned him down. However, to her continuing shame, Kathy Beale dated him for a while. Richard also thinks that he's the toughest, meanest, most feared man in town.

As the local market inspector he has a certain amount of power. He gave Rachel Kominsky a prize pitch because he thought it would get her into bed. It worked, eventually – but no sooner had he bedded her than he moved on to her best friend Kathy. He used his connections at the council to shop Ian's kitchens to the health inspector. Richard would in fact do anything to cause Ian grief, as the two are sworn enemies.

Part of his campaign against Ian included flirting with his wife. Although Cindy encouraged him, Richard pushed things too far and when she rejected him he still told locals that he had slept with her. And later when she was pregnant he did nothing to dispel the rumours – that he had maliciously started – that her twins were his.

He used his influence to get Arthur a job as a street sweeper, but then took great delight in reminding poor old Arthur that he owed him a favour.

Shelley Lewis tried to teach him a lesson when he showed a bit of interest. She flirted with him for perfume, roses and sexy underwear, and he couldn't understand why she wouldn't sleep with him. His wounded pride turned him into even more of a bastard.

When Sanjay and Gita arrived in Albert Square, it became clear that Richard had been responsible for the downfall of Sanjay's thriving import business, underlining the fact that Richard is a cold-blooded creature who would hurt his mates if there was sadistic pleasure in it for him.

The trouble with Richard is that he's not a Londoner, he's a northerner with no sense of East End pride. He doesn't stick up for his mates and he doesn't understand their need to protect their patch. He's constantly out for himself and it's just me, me, me. And he's so cocky and arrogant that he thinks he's invincible.

Tricky Dicky is a very clever man, and he's good at thinking on his feet and coming up with cruel one-liners. But it doesn't take much analysis to realise his insults are insubstantial. Nevertheless he can still cause a lot of pain, and enjoys threatening people with this ability.

Consequently he has few friends and lives alone above the betting shop at 13 Turpin Road. He has few interests other than chasing women, telling himself he's perfect and winding people up.

NICK COTTON — SEE 'DOT AND NICK'

MEHMET OSMAN

Ali's big brother Mehmet gained the title the Terrible Turk for his womanising ways. He was flash, good-looking and lucky. He spent his winnings from poker and the horses on gold jewellery that found a home nestled in his hairy chest.

He could smooth-talk his way round Ali and his wife Guizin. But all that he said was lacking in substance, and he encouraged his brother to follow his example.

Mehmet's most despicable trait was that he truly thought he was better than other people. He had no qualms about using people or ripping people off. He once conned Mary into sleeping with him because Ali had bet him £10 that he couldn't get her into bed. When Mary found out, she kneed him where it hurt! But when Pete found out that he had ripped Kathy off for £2,000, Mehmet got more than he bargained for.

Mehmet had promised Kathy he could sell her hand-made jumpers up West for a lot of money, so she employed Michelle and the two women worked round the clock to meet his client's deadline.

But when they handed over the goods there was no payment in return – Mehmet had flogged them himself. So Pete and his mates decided to give him another flogging, and the Terrible Turk was kicked and punched in Albert Square gardens and he finally had to admit that he was no better than the rest of them.

MANDY SALTER – SEE 'WAIFS AND STRAYS'

JAMES WILLMOTT-BROWN

This ex-army officer was always like a fish out of water in Walford with his upper-crust manner and law-abiding ways. He first appeared in Albert Square in 1986 as the area manager for Luxford and Copley, the brewery that owns the Vic. He was so strait-laced that he queried the tiniest discrepancies in Angie's book-keeping.

It therefore came as quite a surprise when he announced he was resigning from Luxford's (his job was taken over by Mr Sparrow, far more Den's sort of man) and moving to the Square. He bought number 43 off Debbie Wilkins, and then bought the rundown Dagmar pub in Turpin Road and shocked the locals when he said he was the new landlord.

He converted the Dagmar from a mecca for prostitutes and drug dealers into a yuppie heaven. Decorated in classic eighties peppermint with soft lighting and a dance-floor, it signalled the 'yuppiefication' of Albert Square. James came across as very keen to become part of the community, and he gave Arthur a job when he'd just come out of prison; he even gave Mary a job as the pub's cleaner because he wanted her to get back on her feet. But his nice-guy image wasn't going to last for long.

The Dagmar was set to give the Vic a run for its money, especially as James had enlisted Angie as his manageress. He also poached Kathy Beale from the staff of the Vic and it soon became clear that he had ulterior motives for employing Kath.

James made no bones about thinking Kath's hubby Pete was the perfect oik, and although she did little to defend Pete (she knew better than anyone just how much of an oik he was) she certainly had no intentions of being unfaithful to her husband.

But Double Barrel-Brown mis-read the signs, and one night in July 1988 he invited her to his flat upstairs after closing for a drink. He made a pass at her and she fended him off, but he raped her.

Later, when he was arrested, he claimed Kathy had consented. That night his precious pub was torched to the ground and Den was seen gloating as he looked on.

Willmott-Brown refused to accept that he'd done anything wrong; he even offered to take Kathy away from the Square to somewhere where they would be free to express their love for each other! He really, truly thought he had done exactly what Kathy had wanted him to do.

When he finally understood that she was serious about taking him to court he tried to bribe her, but Kathy was smarter than he reckoned and when he went round to

Michelle's to finalise a settlement with Kath, she made sure the police were there to catch him.

This, and the emotional evidence Kathy gave in court, was enough for him to be sent down for three years. His posh accent and his money made it even easier for the locals to hate him. That made his return to Walford in 1992 all the more remarkable. He bought the pizza place round the back of the arches in an auction, and intended to tart the joint up and start all over again.

He had served a year of his sentence and felt he had (unjustly) paid his dues. He wanted to move back to his old house with his kids, Luke and Sophie, and he still wanted Kathy in his life. His infatuation with her bordered on obsession, and even a beating from the locals couldn't make him leave Walford – he wanted to be close to Kathy. In the end, Kathy and her now ex-husband Pete went round to number 43 for a showdown. Kath finally convinced Willmott-Brown that she never cared for him and, more to the point, she absolutely despised him. Pete was finally the man he ought to have been all along and Willmott-Brown was forced to recognise that his only chance for survival was well away from Walford.

JACK WOODMAN — SEE VICKI'S KIDNAP ORDEAL

BIRTHS

Having a baby is never easy, but in Albert Square it's often downright calamitous! Pregnancies are either fraught with complications (often the mother's life is at risk), or the paternity is in doubt, or the birth itself comes at the most inappropriate time.

Babies in Albert Square aren't just the cute and cuddly kind. They cry a lot (who can blame them?), they get ill, or even abandoned. In fact, most of the time babies in Walford mean only one thing – trouble!

MARTIN FOWLER, 1 AUGUST 1985

Poor little Martin, even before he was born he was an inconvenience to his family. His mum Pauline was 42 when she discovered she was pregnant in February 1985, and his dad Arthur had been unemployed for over a year. But despite the risk to both mother and child, Lou's protestations and the family's financial situation, Pauline and Arthur went ahead with the pregnancy and Martin was born in August.

His christening in September had to be postponed because he contracted gastro-enteritis. Pete, Kathy and Den were to be his godparents, but Den – now aware that he was the father of big sister Michelle's unborn child – tried to ditch his new responsibility. Michelle almost blew his cover when she exploded at him in the Vic, accusing him of thinking the Fowlers 'weren't good enough for him', so Den complied. But he was unable to attend the christening and Wicksy stood in as proxy when the christening was eventually held a month later.

Although there was a sixteen-year age gap between Michelle and Martin, the little lad still grew up with a 'sister' his own age. Vicki may technically be Martin's niece, but the two Fowler kids have been brought up more as siblings.

VICKI FOWLER, 27 MAY 1986

Never had a mother been more expectant than sixteen-year-old Michelle Fowler! Just as she was about to set off to school to revise for an O level, the contractions started and she realised she wouldn't be sitting any exams that day! Her uncle Pete drove her and her mum Pauline to Walford General Hospital in his fruit and veg van.

Pauline coaxed her daughter through the labour in the absence of the (secret) father. That evening Arthur and Lou visited, bringing unwanted flowers from Lofty. While Pauline cooed over her first grandchild, and Lou mused about her duties as a great-grandmother, Michelle wondered if her daughter's father would show.

He did. After visiting hours, Den snuck into the ward, kidding the nurse that he was Michelle's godfather who had travelled a long way. It was an emotional meeting and it was an enormous risk to take – what if someone had seen them? But it was a risk worth taking: Den held his only natural child in his arms, and both mother and father were obviously moved by the encounter. It was one of only two times that Den would ever hold his daughter.

ALI OSMAN, 24 MARCH 1988

Named after his father, little Ali was the most loved baby the East End had ever known. His older brother Hassan had died a cot death in June 1985 and his parents Sue and Ali, who ran the café in Bridge Street, had been desperate to replace him.

After Sue's breakdown following the loss of her son,

the mixed-race couple (he was a Turkish Cypriot, she was pure Walford) had tried virtually every method of fertilisation known to medicine, but their lack of success put such a strain on their marriage that they came close to splitting up.

Meanwhile Sue had become obsessive about every other baby in the Square and quickly volunteered for babysitting duty, especially for Annie Smith, the confused toddler of punk Mary.

But Sue and Ali managed to rekindle their romance, and ripped up the calendar that only reminded them of their loss, and tried again. And in October 1987, Sue told Ali that she was pregnant again. Ali reserved his celebrations thinking this pregnancy might be another phantom of Sue's desperation, but it soon became clear that he really would be a father again. Never had a woman fretted so much about her unborn child, and it was all health visitor Carmel Roberts could do to stop Sue from spending the entire nine months lying down.

But for all her exhaustive preparation, D-Day came out of the blue and Sue's contractions took her completely unaware – and in the haste, Lofty and Pauline stood in as midwives!

Sue was so protective of her new son that she wouldn't take him outside for ages for fear that he might catch a bug. Her obsession about little Ali was as destructive as her grief for Hassan, so despite their joy at finally becoming parents again, Sue and Ali were never to be happy together again.

STEVEN BEALE, 26 DECEMBER 1989

While Cindy was puffing and panting her way through the premature delivery, expectant dad Ian could barely contain his excitement. Meanwhile, the baby's real father Simon Wicks was bottling up at the Vic. Although Cindy had told Wicksy that he was the father of her child, he didn't really believe her and the fact that she had gone into unexpected labour made him think that she had been lying about the dates all along.

He reasoned that if the baby was born earlier than Cindy had predicted then the baby must be Ian's. But when the news filtered through back to the Vic that the baby, a boy, was in fact premature, Wicksy realised he had become a father.

Proud 'grandfather' Pete dragged Simon along to the hospital, and while the Beales slapped each other on the back, Cindy dragged Wicksy aside into the ward where their premature son was fighting for his life in an incubator crib and forced him to look at his child.

She told him this was his last chance to stake his claim on the kid, or she would be forced to bring him up as Ian's son forever. Wicksy walked away.

While Cindy and Ian took their time coming up with a name for the kid, Wicksy (who was living with Sharon at the time) brooded about his responsibilities.

When Cindy and Wicksy realised a revealing conversation in the Vic had been overheard, they realised someone else was privy to their secret. They suspected it might have been Sharon, but thankfully it turned out to be Michelle who was the only one who could really understand their dilemma, and she agreed to keep their secret and become baby Steven's godmother.

SHARMILLA KAPOOR, 18 MARCH 1993

Sharmilla's dad Sanjay arrived in Walford a couple of months before her birth and stayed with his old pal Richard Cole. 'Tricky Dicky' made sure Sanjay got a good pitch in the market and he set about building up a thriving clothing trade.

Just as Sanjay seemed to be on the right track, his wife Gita arrived in the Square, eight months pregnant. She wanted to be with her husband again, but this time on her terms. She didn't want him gambling and drinking the

money away and she didn't want to be anyone's lodger –
especially Richard's.

There was great antagonism between Gita and Richard;
all she wanted to do was move into a place of their own.
But Sanjay had lost his £800 deposit to Nigel in a poker
game.

So when the time came, Gita was still under Richard's
roof and they were still arguing when her waters broke.
The baby was coming so fast that there was no time to
wait for an ambulance and Richard had to drive her to
the hospital himself. Eventually he got a message back to
Sanjay in the market, who made it to the maternity ward
just in time.

Having Sanjay and his new family stay soon became
too much for Richard and so he helped Sanjay out with a
deposit so they could move into one of the flats at number
43.

PETER & LUCY BEALE, 9 DECEMBER 1993

Like their big brother Steven, the twins were born two
months premature. Perhaps it was genetic, but their
paternity was also challenged, just like Steven's.

Tricky Dicky had been chasing their mum Cindy for
ages, but she constantly rejected him. So when the news
got out that Cindy was pregnant, he started a rumour that
he was the father just to spite her. And after his experience with Steven and Wicksy four years before, Ian had
every reason to doubt his wife.

Cindy begged Ian to believe her, but when he said he
couldn't trust her, she packed her bags and ordered a taxi
to take her and Steven away from Ian forever. But as the
cab was about to leave the Square, Ian flagged it down
and apologised, saying he'd never let anything come
between them ever again.

Christmas 1993 was a bad time for Ian and his family;
not only were the twins' lives in the balance after their
premature arrival, but the birth had coincided with the

news that their granddad Pete had been killed in a car crash.

The grief was piled up as the twins' lives were in danger for weeks before little Lucy was allowed home. Finally, in mid-January 1994, little Peter was also well enough to be allowed to join the rest of his family in Albert Square.

BUSINESS

Too many cooks usually spoil the broth, but in Albert Square they make a dramatic brew. Walford plays home to so many catering enterprises it's a wonder arsenic isn't on everyone's menu!

There's also been an unusually high density of cab firms, car repairers, gardeners, drinking establishments, and grocery sellers in *EastEnders*. And that's no coincidence – because all the friction between the rivals has led to some wonderfully dramatic confrontations.

When the residents of Albert Square mean business, they are ruthless and unforgiving.

THE MARKET

The hustle and bustle of market life is generally light-hearted and friendly, but when there's a rival in town tempers can get hotter than the stolen goods on Sanjay's stall!

Like the time Laurie Bates started a fruit and veg stall in Turpin Road. It was bad enough that he was in direct competition with Pete, but when he started dating Pete's ex-wife Kathy things got out of hand.

The fruit and veg stall at the end of Bridge Street has been in the Beale family for generations, and if Pete ever had to nip into the Vic for a pint, then a relation was sure to be around to mind his tomatoes. Pete was going to fight for his pitch and his honour, and when Laurie started selling festive Christmas trees as well, he could contain his ire no longer.

A bitter cost-cutting battle ensued, until both men were

eventually forced to concede a draw or face bankruptcy. The customers were soon to return to Pete anyway when Laurie left after his split from Kathy.

Pete's stall has since been handed over to his nephew Mark Fowler who thought he'd only be doing the job for a couple of weeks while Pete was on holiday. But when Pete didn't return from his break, Mark realised he had reluctantly inherited the family business. Nevertheless he has made a go of the fruit and veg stall and seems quite at ease with the early starts and London winters.

Another of the Beale clan had a stall for a while. Kathy got a regular pitch in Turpin Road to sell her handmade cardigans and jumpers, but was later tempted back to an indoor job as a barmaid.

The market meant so much to the family that when the Council threatened to close it in 1990, Pete was the one who led the passionate resistance.

His followers in the successful mission were the market regulars who are always around to help out if they're needed. There's Lil, who runs a clothes stall, and Maude, who has a wagon of second-hand books. If Big Ron's not on his hardware stall, he's probably having another pint of Churchill's in the Vic. And if you're running late for a date, you can always pick up a bunch of flowers from Tracy's stall.

A few years back there was a record stall in Turpin Road, run by Barry Clark, Colin's boyfriend. When he left Walford he handed control over to poet punk Rod Norman, who in turn let Donna Ludlow take over when he moved on.

New faces keep popping up in the market. One of the newest stall-holders is Sanjay Kapoor who keeps a plot across Bridge Street from Mark, selling cheap designer clobber.

In 1992, Richard Cole started displaying his peacock feathers as the market's new inspector. He uses his influence to win women and keep blokes one favour behind. He takes his job very seriously (mainly because it's his way of exerting power over the market tenants) but he's not impartial to the odd bribe. An offer of extra cash will get you a long way into Tricky Dicky's good books. And if you're a woman, an offer of dinner will take you all the way! But Tricky Dicky was finally forced into submission when the traders joined forces in December 1993 to insist that he give Big Ron his stall back after a near-fatal heart attack.

CATERING

Time was when all you could get for lunch in Walford was a cheese roll from Ali's café. But times have changed and now you can get everything from cordon bleu cuisine in Kathy's Bistro to a pie and mash in the Queen Vic.

You can also pick up a pre-packed sandwich in First Til Last, a bag of chips from Turpin Road Chippie or a Chinese takeaway from the Green Lantern on the corner. But if you really want something special, Ian Beale will prepare you something mouth-watering and his catering company will come to your house to serve it.

In fact Ian has been involved in most of the catering ventures in *EastEnders* because not only is he a great chef, but he's also an astute businessman. Before he left college he helped Sue and Ali out in the café, but after he'd got his City and Guilds, the Vic and the Dagmar both wanted him to take care of their catering. Ian also got a third offer from Magda Czajkowski, Den's girlfriend at the time and owner of Symphony Foods, a private catering company.

Although Ian took the job at the Vic spicing up shepherd's pies, he was sure to learn all he could from Mags. And after a stint as the owner of the café because Ali couldn't repay his debts, Ian branched out and started local deliveries. Beales on Wheels supplied plenty of local hostelries with lunches and buffets. Ian decided there was more money in private catering and decided to sell the café. He offered it to his auntie Pauline, his mum Kathy and Frank Butcher. When they said they were all interested in buying it, Ian let them up their offers to see what he could get. But they rumbled Ian's ungentlemanly plan and got together a consortium with a third stake each.

While Ian went from strength to strength with his new company the Meal Machine, Kathy, Pauline and their silent partner Frank were having troubles at the café. The relationship between Kath and Pauline had always been volatile, and when Kath thought her former sister-in-law wasn't pulling her weight, she made no bones about telling her.

Kath raised the money to buy Pauline out and enough for a lick of paint, and reopened the joint as a traditional East End café in the day but a cosy French bistro at night. Mrs Weung Cheung used to help her out in the day, but when she retired her eccentric niece Sylvia took over. In the evening she had Arthur's lady friend Christine Hewitt making use of her adult education classes in French cooking. But even with the help, Kath still had to work very long, draining hours.

Her son Ian was also employing staff. He took on bright school leaver Hattie Tavernier as his office assistant and Mark's friend Joe as a chef. But when Ian learnt that Joe was HIV positive he fired him and took on Steve Elliot, a talented chef with designs on Hattie.

Steve found working for Ian insufferable and moved on, angering Ian further by poaching the Vic's lunch-time contract with a lower bid. But the Meal Machine faltered without Steve, and as Hattie was happier with him than without, Steve was offered his old job back on a fairer basis.

The recession eventually took its toll on the Meal Machine, and Ian had to lay Steve off and reduce Hattie's hours. Steve played safe and secured a job on a cruise, adding to Hattie's heartache.

Ian started working from home, and although his new operation was more modest than his last, it was still too adventurous to break even, and he was forced to take a job back at the café helping his mum out.

And even though Kathy has also been forced to down-scale and close the bistro, you can be sure that there'll always be something cooking in Albert Square!

BOOZE

The Vic used to be Queen of all the local drinking establishments, far enough away from friendly rivals the Feathers and the Rose and Crown for them not to be a distraction to the regulars.

But then Naima started selling alcohol in the grocery store, the Dagmar reopened, Strokes wine bar started serving in Turpin Road and for a time even the café had a BYO licence.

When Naima opened up her off-licence section in 1986, Den fretted about the effect on the Vic's trade. But he needn't have worried; plenty of Walfordians were willing to pay to see him and Angie sling their mud (you couldn't get that sort of entertainment at home!).

When Willmott-Brown opened up the Dagmar on the other side of the bridge, Den had a more serious reason to worry. The Dagmar offered a bit of sophistication and a dance floor, and it had Angie pulling the pints. It was a body blow to the Vic's evening trade, but Den managed to hold on to the lunch-time punters with some traditional pub grub.

The rivalry was still fierce however, and the two pubs did battle over the London In Bloom competition and five-a-side football.

When he finally left the Vic in 1988, Den's connections with the Firm set him up in Stokes wine bar in Turpin Road. He was little more than a glorified bouncer; the real business was left to glamorous Joanna who was there to keep her well-mascara'd eye on 'business'. The trade – mostly villains – did little to raise the tone of the neighbourhood, and as the wine bar wasn't quite the right scene for the Pete Beales of this world, Strokes posed little threat to the Vic's new guv'nors Pat and Frank.

These days, with princess Sharon behind the bar, the Vic is once again the jewel of the Square, and the old dear is still seeing off the competition.

CARS

EastEnders' first cab firm was the brainchild of Mehmet Osman. He managed to persuade his pliable brother Ali that with a dodgy old Cortina and a trestle table in the back of the café, they'd be able to set up a viable cab company.

Remarkably they did it! Ozcabs hired new drivers, acquired Den's Rover and went from strength to strength. Typically Mehmet had little to do with the day-to-day running of the operation – he always had something more glamorous to do. And as Sue would rather babysit than man the controls, Ali was the one who made Ozcabs a success. But when Sue's health deteriorated and she had to be admitted into a mental hospital, Ali found he couldn't cope. He gambled to try and make ends meet but ended up losing the café as well.

He went to work for Frank Butcher at the car lot across the Square selling second-hand motors. Ali soon left Walford to return to Cyprus, but Frank's business didn't really need his help anyway. Frank had the gift of the gab to sell the cars and Pat to do his books, and soon he'd have his son Ricky as a mechanic.

But first Ricky had to qualify, and he served his apprenticeship with Phil and Grant Mitchell at their repair shop under the arches. The brothers gave Ricky the job because he was cheap, and because he was a long way short of being smart enough to cotton on to their dodgy deals.

Frank's missus Pat decided that she would start her own company after she'd had to let go of the B&B at number 20. Realising that there was now a gap in the market following Ali's departure, she started PatCabs and manned the radio from Frank's portakabin.

Frank was not best pleased, thinking it was a very unwomanly occupation for his wife – and anyway, he could do it better. Pat asked him to prove it and for a week they swapped jobs! Frank did the school run, and Pat enticed the bargain hunters convincing them that a beat-up Mini was as good as a brand-new Mercedes!

Unsurprisingly, Pat was better at selling cars than Frank was at putting up with a minivan full of screaming kids, and so Pat gained her husband's full co-operation and approval.

The status quo was suddenly demolished at Christmas 1992 when Pat knocked down and killed 22-year-old Stephanie Watson. Pat had been ever so slightly over the blood alcohol limit and could not forgive herself. She would never get in a car again, let alone drive a cab for a living. Frank did his best to help his wife through the ordeal, and he thought that setting up a new firm, F And P Cabs, would be a solid start. But Pat railed against his meddling, and it wasn't until she had been released from prison that she could bear to act as radio controller again.

But that proved to be just as dangerous as driving the London streets, for a rival cab firm subjected F&P to a hate campaign. After a cruel and intimidating attack on Pat in the portakabin, Frank conceded and agreed to close the firm down. And even though that decision led to great financial hardship, Pat was more than relieved.

DEATHS

The folk of Albert Square have been touched by the heartache of losing a loved one more times than seems fair. Murder, cot-death, suicide, AIDS – *EastEnders* has seen it all.

The show's very first scene was in Reg Cox's bedsit where his lifeless body was discovered by Den, Arthur and Ali. He had been savagely beaten and robbed.

Since then more than ten other East Enders have met their maker. One thing's for sure – if you intend on living a long life, don't move to Albert Square!

REG COX, 19 FEBRUARY 1985

When Reg hadn't been in to pick up his pint of milk for the third day in a row, shopkeepers Naima and Saeed Jeffrey were concerned. They asked around and found no one had seen him for days.

The East End, being the tight-knit community that it is, took it upon itself to investigate. Local publican Den Watts enlisted Arthur Fowler's help to go and check out Reg's room at Number 23 Albert Square.

Ali Osman, who lived in the room beneath Reg, let them into the building and went upstairs with them while he was still wearing his pyjamas. When Reg didn't answer his door, Den kicked it in and the three men saw their elderly neighbour slumped in an armchair.

'Stinks in 'ere,', Den noted as Arthur discovered the half-empty whisky bottle. They opened the curtains and let the sun highlight the squalor Reg had been living in. Dr Legg was summoned and an ambulance was called. Reg was still alive, just.

Nosy neighbours looked on as the old boy was taken to hospital, where he died. Gossip as good as this spread round the Square like wildfire, and pretty soon Reg's demise was on everybody's lips.

By all accounts, Reg Cox was a cantankerous old sod who drank too much and was rude to just about everyone. So when the news filtered through that he'd passed on, it was clear he wasn't going to be missed.

The police suspected that Reg had been murdered and an inquiry was launched immediately. Suspect Number One was layabout Mark Fowler, but no one escaped suspicion.

Reg's death and subsequent finger-pointing was a field day for the local gossips, and all the old-timers warbled on about how it would never had happened in the good old days.

When Lofty and Mark were both found in possession of Reg's old war medals, they were questioned and it transpired that it was Nick Cotton who had sold them to the lads. Nick was now under scrutiny as the possible murderer, but the police never gathered enough information to convict him – even though everyone knew he was guilty.

The locals were proved right when Nick finally confessed the crime to Den when they were in prison together in December of 1988.

HASSAN OSMAN, 20 JUNE 1985

At 7.30 in the morning, a little later than usual because her nine-month-old son Hassan usually roused her with his crying, Sue woke up.

She kissed her husband Ali as he slept soundly after celebrating a gambling win the night before. As she went to check on Hassan she saw immediately that he was dead. Too shocked to even touch her son, she called for her husband. 'Ali,' she croaked. 'Ali.' He woke and rushed over to the cot and started shaking Hassan. It was too early to call Dr Legg, so they grabbed their son and rushed across the Square to the only other medical professional they knew – Andy O'Brien.

Andy was already dressed and was about to leave for work when the Osmans started banging on his door. Next-door neighbour Pauline Fowler saw the commotion when she picked up her milk from her doorstep and wondered what was happening.

Andy and Debs took control of the situation. She phoned for Dr Legg, an ambulance and Ali's brother while Andy tried to resuscitate the tot, knowing full well that his efforts were in vain.

When the medics arrived they shielded Sue and Ali from Hassan as if he was no longer theirs. When Hassan was pronounced dead, Ali flopped and demanded Dr Legg to tell him that it was a mistake. Sue meanwhile had gone numb, staring inanely into the middle distance. If she was told to drink a cup of tea she would drink it, if she was told to sit down, she did. When the doctors asked her simple questions like Hassan's date of birth, she could not answer. The shock had wiped her memory clean.

Ali's family arrived and suddenly the scene of shock turned into one of grief. They started wailing in Turkish, leaving Sue in English isolation. Ali and his brothers accompanied Hassan to the hospital for the post-mortem, while Sue stayed motionless at Debs and Andy's. Debbie tried to comfort her, but all Sue could say was that she was worried about who would do the rolls for the lunches at the Vic.

When Ali returned from the hospital, the scenes of grief continued, but Sue couldn't cry. She couldn't even move and she stayed in Debs and Andy's living room for days before she was finally persuaded to go back to her own home.

The whole Square went into shock. Michelle and Lofty helped out at the café, Andy was a tower of strength, and everyone did everything they could to ease Sue's pain.

She became obsessive about kids and would babysit readily whenever there was an opportunity. So desperate was she to replace Hassan that she even had a psychological phantom pregnancy. Her dream of becoming a mother again finally came true in March 1988, when she gave birth to little Ali.

ANDY O'BRIEN, 14 AUGUST 1986

Everybody loved Andy O'Brien. He was one of Albert Square's original good Samaritans. When he helped Mary learn to read, she misinterpreted his concern, and when he comforted Angie over Den's philanderings she too took advantage of the kindly Scot.

Andy moved to the Square in 1985 with his girlfriend, uptight bank clerk Debbie Wilkins. The two had a tempestuous relationship and they were both tempted to infidelity. But after she refused Sergeant Quick's marriage proposal and he ended his fling with Angie, it looked like they were finally setting sail for a happy future together.

However, they still argued about money. Like the time he'd forgotten to post their insurance payments and they were then cruelly burgled. Her banking training made her intolerant of foolishness with money. So when she learnt he'd lent Wicksy money for some musical equipment, a bitchy row erupted. It ended with Andy storming out as he was late for work and Debbie telling him to 'drop dead'.

Her words were prophetic. On his way to the hospital where he was a male nurse, he saw an out-of-control lorry heading straight for a careless toddler. In one final act of heroism, Andy dived in front of the lorry to push the kid out of the way and was killed.

Debs was distraught. Everywhere she turned she saw lookalikes, and her final words to him haunted her. As only a live-in lover, she had no claim on Andy and no say in his funeral arrangements. Still, she took comfort from the knowledge that even in death he had been a hero – Andy had carried a donor card and his kidneys saved someone else's life.

In time she recovered well enough to marry a detective sergeant, but not Roy Quick; she eventually fell for the thuggish Terry Rich.

TOM CLEMENTS, 21 APRIL 1988

Tom, it has to be said, was a bit of a miser. He would work in the Vic collecting empty glasses all afternoon for a free pint at the end of it, rather than shell out any of his own money.

He also worked as the caretaker at the community centre behind Bridge Street. Tom was a war veteran who felt he never really got the thanks he deserved for protecting his country, and he never ceased of harping on about it.

He had a tendency to take things too seriously. When he was doing the Vic's flowers for the London In Bloom contest, he declared war on his main rival Arthur Fowler, who was designing the Dagmar's display. That's not to say Tom didn't have any compassion. He gladly swapped houses with Dot and Ethel so they could share his larger house. Of course, living in a bedsit meant Tom could keep his costs down, but nevertheless, he still expected to be thanked profusely for his gesture.

So it should come as no surprise to learn that Tom died of a heart attack. This man's pent-up stress had been building for years. And one day while pot-clearing in the Vic, he nipped into the gents'. When Den popped in to relieve himself he found Tom's lifeless body.

No one in the Square missed Tom, but Dot thought it was her Christian duty to attend his funeral. Sadly, she was the only mourner.

LOU BEALE, 21 JULY 1988

It was typical of Walford's wise old woman to know exactly when she was going to die. The old girl had been failing for a while – she'd had to move into the front room in 1985 because she couldn't manage the stairs, but for her the greater indignity was having to use a commode.

Although her body started to feel its age, Lou's brain was still razor-sharp. One night she called a family conference and summoned every Beale and Fowler. There was no particular crisis that needed dealing with, and everyone was bemused at Lou's behaviour. She was doling out beloved keepsakes and warm advice. She asked her brood to bury hatchets and be good to each other, before retiring to bed.

The next morning, Pauline took breakfast in to her mum. She returned to the lounge moments later saying simply, 'She's gone.'

A funeral was quickly arranged and Duncan the curate held a beautiful service (even if he did call her 'Louisa' rather than 'Louise'). Even those that loathed the old battleaxe turned out to show their last respects. Everyone knew that Albert Square wouldn't be the same without her.

The loss was hardest on Pete, but even he managed to choke back his tears and toast the 'bloody old bag' in the Vic on the night of the service.

Lou's picture is still on the wall in the Fowlers' house, but her presence is felt more sharply when Pauline emulates her mother's wisdom and interfering. Michelle, too, will one day be another Lou.

DENNIS WATTS, 23 FEBRUARY 1989

It has never been confirmed that Den did actually die on that fateful afternoon in February 1989, typical of Den to keep us guessing!

He had been banged up on remand in Dickens Hill prison for the torching of the Dagmar, and on his way to trial he was kidnapped by the Firm who wanted to stop him from testifying for fear he would double-cross them.

But Den, fearing for his life, managed to escape. He

was in the middle of nowhere with nowhere to hide – and he desperately needed an ally. While the Firm staked out Sharon and Michelle's flat at number 43, Den called there from a phone box. First Sharon answered the phone, and Den put the receiver down at the sound of her voice – she would be too emotional and be no use at all.

The next time Den tried to make contact, Pauline picked up. The look of disgust on his face said it all – there was no way he was going to trust her in his hour of need.

Thankfully, the third time he called, Michelle answered. Talking in a half-code, Den asked Michelle to bring Vicki to see him and they arranged to meet at the usual place, but Michelle – sensing danger? – left Vicki at home. Mantel, the Firm's boss, had instructed that Sharon was to be followed everywhere in case Den tried to make contact. But when he saw how Michelle reacted at the mention of Den's name, he had her followed too, just in case.

If Michelle ever knew that it was her indiscretion that led to Den's downfall she would never forgive herself. But as she made her way to the canal for their last veiled meeting, she was being shadowed by two gunmen.

She met Den and they sat and talked. He said he had to go away, but that he wanted the women in his life, Michelle, Sharon and Vicki, to know that he wasn't deserting them. He promised he would make contact when he could. Yet again Michelle vowed to keep his secrets and the pair parted, leaving in opposite directions. As Michelle walked away she passed a man walking a dog. He was concealing a gun beneath his jacket. Den, walking in the opposite direction noticed a couple walking arm in arm; the guy was carrying a bunch of daffodils. Den smiled – he thought he had escaped the Firm. But a look in the eye of the man carrying the flowers made him panic; he turned around to see the dog walker aiming a gun at him, and as Den turned back a gun concealed in the daffodils fired a single shot. A splash was heard and it seemed Den had fallen into the canal.

The police started searching for Den when he didn't show for trial, but Michelle didn't worry because Den had told her he would lie low. So when the boys in blue explained to her and Sharon that an informer had told them Den had been murdered, she was shocked. She protested so vehemently that she almost let it be known he was Vicki's dad.

A year later, a body that was thought to be Den's was fished out of the canal several miles downstream. Sharon was so upset that she ran away and left Michelle to organise the funeral. However, the identity of the body was never proved beyond doubt, and so it's just possible that Den's biding his time before he lets it be known that he's still alive. And maybe one day, he'll walk back into the Vic and order a pint of Churchill's.

DONNA LUDLOW, 13 APRIL 1989

Donna came to the Square in 1987 and got a job as a barmaid at the Vic. From the start it was clear she was unbalanced, telling stories about her parents and her exotic childhood in Canada. Or was it Australia? Donna was a compulsive liar, and her stories never added up.

The one tale she didn't tell, however, was how she'd come to the Square to get close to her natural mother, Kathy Beale. Kath had given birth to Donna – the product of a vicious rape – when she was fourteen and done her best to forget about her. Donna used all her evil cunning to worm her way into Kathy's affections (including seducing her genetic half-brother Ian), but that deceit only made Kathy reject her more when she learned the truth. 'You and me are strangers, Donna. We come from different worlds,' Kathy told her. 'Just leave it as it is, yeah?'

Kath's rejection was the tip of a slippery slope for Donna, and when Donna learnt the truth about her conception she turned to heroin for comfort and justification of her existence. At the time she'd been squatting with Rod in Colin's old flat at number 3. She had tried to blackmail everyone in the Square and she was lucky that Rod had some sympathy left for her. When even he had had enough, only Dot and her Christian charity would take her in. The drugs served to heighten Donna's delusions further and when she bumped into Kath in the market and they fell into each other's arms, Donna thought maybe Kath had come to accept her.

Kathy agreed to talk, and in Pete's lock-up next to the Vic she explained that she never asked for Donna and that she didn't owe her anything.

Donna lost all faith in living at that point and went home to Dot's to take an overdose. When Dot returned to her house that night she found Donna sprawled on her living room floor. She had choked to death on her own vomit.

CHARLIE COTTON, 10 JULY 1991 – SEE 'DOT AND NICK'

EDDIE ROYLE, 10 SEPTEMBER 1991

It was Roly who first alerted the Square that there was something wrong. When Dot heard him barking she rushed outside, and found the Vic's guv'nor Eddie Royle lying in the middle of Albert Square gardens with a fatal stab wound through his heart.

A murder investigation was started and the immediate suspects were the unstable and violent Grant Mitchell (who had hospitalised Eddie once before), and Clyde Tavernier, who had recently been seen arguing with Eddie.

So when Nick Cotton told the cops that he had seen Clyde from his bedroom window standing over Eddie's body with a knife in his hand, the police were only too happy to arrest him.

Clyde, knowing full well that he was innocent, went on

110

the run, fearing he was the victim of a racist investigation. Meanwhile, 'wanted' posters went up all over Walford for his arrest.

Several months later, Nick confessed to his mum that he had in fact committed the crime by escaping from his bedroom where he had been detoxifying from his heroin dependency. Dot wrestled with her conscience, but knew she had to shop her only son to the police, and so Clyde was let off the hook. However, at the subsequent trial, the jury decided there was not enough evidence to convict Nick, and so for the second time he got away with murder.

GILL FOWLER, 25 JUNE 1992

Gill's death from an HIV-related cancer was confusing and heartbreaking for her husband of one day, Mark Fowler. Mark, a carrier of HIV himself, had fallen deeply in love with his former girlfriend as he cared for her through the end of her illness. To show this love, he arranged for her to be taken out of the hospice to the local registry office where they exchanged vows. That night they dined with Michelle, and Mark's former girlfriend Rachel, to celebrate, and ate a meal of ice-cream sundaes because that was all Gill could manage.

Gill tired quickly, and so Mark took her to their honeymoon suite to rest, but he soon noticed that the excitement had been too much for his bride and he called for an ambulance to take Gill back to the hospice.

The next day he waited at his wife's bedside for the inevitable. Gill look skinny and tired, her eyes were shady hollows and every breath was an effort.

George, Gill's nurse, warned Mark that 'this could be it'. Mark demanded that he do something, 'Give her an injection or something,' but George calmed him down and persuaded him that the best thing he could do for Gill now was to tell her that he loved her.

So Mark returned to her room and did as he was told. 'Love you, Gill,' he said. 'I'm glad I met you.'

Gill opened her eyes and looked at her husband for the last time. She cracked a joke – 'It's been fun, hasn't it?' – and with a half-smile she drifted away. Mark, disbelievingly, looked on. After a while he asked of George, 'Is that it?'

'Yeah,' said George. 'That's it.'

Gill's death affected Mark deeply – he knew that one day he would die of the same illness. And as he knew how painful it was, he didn't know if he could take it. He turned to alcohol for a while, but in time he made his peace with his fate, and Mark is now one of the wisest and most reasonable people in *EastEnders*.

STEPHANIE WATSON, 24 DECEMBER 1992 –
SEE 'TRAGEDY AND TRAUMA'

MO BUTCHER, 24 DECEMBER 1992 –
SEE 'THE BUTCHERS'

PETE BEALE, 9 DECEMBER 1993 –
SEE 'THE BEALES AND THE FOWLERS'

DIVORCE

It seems quite ironic that there have been so many extra-marital affairs in *EastEnders*, but not once has an affair led to divorce, or has one mistress subsequently become a wife.

That's because divorce in Albert Square comes about not out of spite or retaliation, but quite simply because couples involved had simply married the wrong partner in the first place. There has never been a big custody battle or rows over child support, but that doesn't mean divorce has ever been easy . . .

SAEED AND NAIMA JEFFREY, DECEMBER 1985

Naima was never happy in her role as a traditional Muslim wife, and it was clear that Saeed would never be man enough for her. She had only married him to get her family off her back. Before the marriage she told Saeed that she wouldn't sleep with him, and he consented, thinking that she would learn to love him. And anyway, she would realise it was her duty.

But Naima did not comply to tradition, and Saeed got increasingly more frustrated. He visited prostitutes and started making obscene phone calls to several of the women round the Square. At Christmas 1985, Naima asked her husband for a divorce. Out of pride, Saeed tried to fight her wishes, but in the end had to concede that the marriage had no future and emigrated to Bangladesh where he remarried.

Naima meanwhile was being sent a series of cousins

that her family wanted to pair her off with. She rejected the cocky Rezaul, but to her surprise found Farrukh quite charming, and in July 1987, she left Albert Square to marry him in Bangladesh.

DEN AND ANGIE WATTS, MAY 1987 – SEE 'AFFAIRS' AND 'DEN AND ANGIE'

TONY AND HANNAH CARPENTER, MAY 1987

Hannah was the china doll to Tony's teddy bear, but unfortunately for these star-crossed lovers they didn't live in Toy Town. They had to make do with Albert Square where reality throws a harsh light on trouble.

They were never able to live with each other even though they were ever so fond of each other. Hannah finally left Tony in the early 1980s because she wanted a man she could be proud of. Tony, she realised, was never going to change; he would always be an amiable handyman, and she wanted a more advanced model.

She found Neville Agard, a sophisticated city slicker. She moved in with him, taking her twelve-year-old daughter Cassie with her. Her seventeen-year-old son Kelvin lived with Tony at number 3. But Neville turned out to be violent, and when he started bullying Cassie too, it was Tony that Hannah ran to. He was happy to help his wife, and they agreed to try to live together as a family again – but in separate flats! Tony and Kelvin would continue to live in the basement, while Hannah and her daughter moved into one of the conversions upstairs.

But Albert Square was too drab for Hannah, and soon her affection for Tony turned to fury as he refused to 'better' himself. Tony, in turn, got tired of her nagging.

The couple agreed they had no future together and planned a divorce. Tony also realised he had no future in

Britain and in May 1987 he returned to his native Trinidad.

MICHELLE AND LOFTY HOLLOWAY, APRIL 1988

In the end, Michelle had only married Lofty out of guilt because she had jilted him previously. And although she hoped she would grow to love him, in her heart of hearts she knew they had no future together.

Lofty bored her. He was so desperate to make sure he wasn't disappointing her that he trailed her like Mary's little lamb, and in the end he smothered her. Michelle's instinctive reaction was to push him away. Lofty's reaction was to suggest that they have a child of their own.

Michelle wasn't so keen, but she somehow felt that she owed Lofty his own kid, and agreed to try for a baby. But at eighteen, the thought of a second baby made her feel even more trapped and she offered to run away with Den. She backtracked when she realised that Lofty was a better man than Den could ever be.

In December 1987, Michelle discovered she was pregnant again, but she knew that having the baby would only tie her to Lofty for life and she resolved to have an abortion, which Den paid for. While she was in the clinic, Pauline did some damaging meddling and told Lofty about the baby.

Michelle, clutching her aching belly, returned to face him, but Lofty had no sympathy left. He called her a murderer and threw her and her belongings out on the street. Michelle moved back to Pauline's and she did her best to make her mum feel guilty for meddling.

Lofty left the Square the following April to work at a children's home in the Home Counties. A simple divorce was arranged through solicitors, and although Michelle seemed to have left the marriage emotionally intact. Lofty hadn't. His final message to Walford came in a card he sent to Michelle on what would have been the birthday of

the child she aborted. 'You may have forgotten,' it read.
'But I never will.'

There was a time when it was inconceivable that Pete and
Kathy would split up. In the mid-eighties they were
Walford's happiest couple. They didn't have the money
worries of Pauline and Arthur, or the infidelity of Den
and Angie, and their son Ian gave them few problems.

Kathy was Pete's second wife, whom he'd married as
soon as he'd got divorced from Pat. She was only seventeen and Pete was her first serious boyfriend, but against
the odds they had made their marriage work.

But in December 1985, the cracks started to show when
Kathy revealed that she had been pregnant as a result of
a rape and had had a daughter when she was fourteen.
Pete was furious that his wife had kept such a secret from
him, and instead of being sympathetic to Kathy's teenage
misery, behaved as if he was the one that had been
wronged.

Their age gap started to show when he wanted to stay
and watch TV and she wanted to get glammed up and
spend a night out with her mates. Pete disapproved of
Kathy getting a job at the Dagmar, because it wasn't the
sort of place that 'their kind of people' went to. But
against his will, Kathy took the job anyway.

This led Pete to think that something was going on
between Kathy and her new boss James Willmott-Brown.
And when James started flirting with Kath, Pete felt fully
vindicated. Pete's pompous behaviour only pushed Kath
into spending more time at work, which succeeded in
further persuading the lecherous Willmott-Brown that
Kathy really felt something for him.

After Willmott-Brown raped Kathy in January 1988,
Pete couldn't be convinced that she hadn't 'asked for it',
and he showed his wife little sympathy. Pete's bull-

headedness made Kathy realise that she didn't really want to be with him. She certainly didn't want to sleep with him, a rejection that Pete saw as an insult to his East End machismo.

The new year was going to be a new start for Kathy and in January 1989 she told Pete that their marriage was over and she moved out of their council flat at 14b Walford Towers. Pete took the news badly and in a drunken fury he crashed Mehmet's car. He still carried a torch for Kath, even though she told him there was no future for them. Not that she was interested in anyone else – she was still too disturbed by Willmott-Brown to think about sleeping with another man.

However, in September she met Laurie Bates, who, coincidentally, was another fruit and veg man! After much gentle persuading the couple finally made love, but Kathy still ended the relationship a few months later.

Seeing Kathy with someone else made Pete realise that their marriage was really over, and when he met a woman called Barbara while on holiday in New Zealand he knew he could have feelings for someone else too. After that, it was just a matter of time before their divorce became a formality.

PAT AND BRIAN WICKS, MAY 1989

Pat had married Brian after Pete divorced her in the mid-sixties. But by all accounts theirs wasn't a very stable marriage and they had both felt free to see other people. There was therefore little urgency to get divorced when they went their separate ways.

It wasn't until Pat wanted to marry Frank in 1989 that it became necessary for her to make the split legal. Brian was a wily and cunning man who cared little for Pat's feelings, and he realised he had a chance to get something out of a divorce. He knew that Frank ran a car lot and so Brian dug his heels in and said he would only grant Fat Pat a divorce if she got him a motor.

As Pat was desperate to make the break she consented, knowing full well that Frank would never agree to the idea. So she told her future husband that she wanted to give her elderly Aunty Mabel a car to help her get around. Frank, thinking it was a lovely idea, offered her a brown Mini.

Brian had been expecting something a bit more flash, but as she had kept her end of the bargain she forced Brian to do the same, and the solicitors were called in to do the necessary.

CARMEL AND MATTHEW JACKSON, JULY 1989

Matthew was white and Carmel was black, but race was not going to be an issue in their relationship – it was love that counted. Matthew moved into his health visitor girlfriend's flat at number 3 in September 1988, and it seemed everything was perfect – so perfect in fact that Matthew asked Carmel to marry him. And she accepted. Even when they were lumbered with looking after Carmel's niece and nephew, this modern couple seemed to cope.

Things started to go wrong when Carmel surprised her fiancé by inviting his mum to their wedding in January 1989. He was not amused and the marriage got off to a poor start. When Carmel's dad had a stroke, she was required to take care of Junior and Ayisha full time. At this point Matthew's temper started to surface. It transpired that the model husband had some deep-seated problems and a tendency to fly off the handle and get violent.

Carmel bore the brunt of this violence in May, when Matthew flipped after she teased him about something trivial. She resolved to give him a chance, she wanted to help him, and she made excuses for the bruises and it was never mentioned again. His violence resurfaced after she'd had a working lunch with Dr David Samuels, and

118

Matthew got worked up into a jealous frenzy. In the fight that followed, Matthew ended up getting stabbed by Junior with a kitchen knife. Carmel realised her marriage had no future and threw Matthew out. She started divorce proceedings and left the Square shortly afterwards to take care of her sick father.

ISSUES

Life in Albert Square is a series of events that seem to come straight from newspaper headlines. Nothing misses the folk of Albert Square, and Walford has seen all the scourges life can offer, except maybe a biblical plague of locusts.

Teen pregnancy, drugs, AIDS, racism, drunk driving – *EastEnders* has seen it all.

ABORTION

It's never an easy decision for any woman, but several of Albert Square's residents have gone through the traumatic process of terminating a pregnancy.

It's not something that Dot would ever have liked her neighbours to know, but against her Christian principles she was forced to have a termination by her husband Charlie in their first year of marriage. She had been ecstatic at the thought of having a child, but Charlie was adamant that he was not going to support a child and told Dot that if she had the baby he would leave her.

So when she was just 21 she went to a back-street abortionist to give up her dream of motherhood. In the end, Charlie left her anyway.

The decision was far more clear cut for Michelle Fowler when she found out she was pregnant by her hapless husband Lofty Holloway. She knew in her heart of hearts that her marriage had no future. She was eighteen and trapped by circumstances to life with a kid, a marriage and a pokey bedsit. She knew that having the baby would mean she would never be free, and so she decided to have

120

the abortion without even telling Lofty that she was pregnant.

So determined was she to get rid of the child that she couldn't wait for the NHS waiting list to clear, so she got Den to pay for her to go private. She wanted to shut out the problem and forget it, so when she was offered the option of a local or general anaesthetic for the operation, she elected to be put out for the count. But when she came round she still had to face telling a broken-hearted Lofty of her deed, because Pauline had thought it her duty to tell him about the pregnancy.

Although she never knew, it transpired that Michelle's future landlady Rachel Kominsky had also faced a similar dilemma. The two women never knew that they had shared the same secret. Rachel got pregnant when she was just fourteen, still at an age where she could be bossed around by her overbearing Jewish mother. Appalled at her daughter's blossoming womanhood (and disgusted by her shameful early introduction to sex) she forced Rachel to terminate her pregnancy. And Rachel was always left wondering about what might have been.

Etta Tavernier had decided she didn't want any more children – her career was taking off and she couldn't take the risk – and so she decided to be sterilised. But when she went to the doctor's for a consultation she was presented with the shock news that she was already pregnant.

Confused, she didn't know what to do, so she turned to her husband Celestine for advice. He was thrilled at the thought of becoming a father again – a baby might just be what they needed to bring them closer and save the marriage. But Etta had an offer of a job as a headmistress and she knew a baby would be a barrier in her career. However, Celestine badgered her and persuaded her not to have an abortion. But when tests showed that the baby had sickle-cell anaemia, like their youngest son Lloyd, she knew she didn't want to put another child through that agony. So she had an abortion against her family's wishes.

Lloyd took it to mean that she had regretted having him, and Celestine thought her actions were un-Christian and unforgivable.

Her daughter Hattie also decided to have an abortion a few years later in 1993. She had been engaged to the father, Steve Elliot, but Steve was having second thoughts about the marriage and ran off before she had had a chance to tell him about her expectant state.

She followed him to Southampton, where he had a job on a cruise ship, seeking an explanation for his disappearance. But he treated her so badly that she didn't tell him about the baby – she wanted him to want her for herself and not because of notions of responsibility.

So she returned to Albert Square and started making plans to have the baby on her own. But friends and family persuaded her that the sacrifice she was making to her career was too great.

Michelle Fowler stepped in and offered the name and number of a clinic that 'a friend of hers' had used. When Hattie asked to meet this friend, Michelle confessed that it was her, and Hattie decided to go through with the operation.

She went to the clinic with her brother's girlfriend Gidea, but after a lengthy conversation, Hattie decided against the abortion.

As she was in the Vic finally celebrating her pregnancy, she was crippled by a searing pain and sadly miscarried.

AIDS

HIV and AIDS first got mentioned in Albert Square when Colin Russell's boyfriend Barry Clark worried that his flu was a symptom of infection. He decided to get a blood test and spent a week preoccupied and brooding until the result came through that he was in the clear.

AIDs didn't really touch the heart of Walford until 1990, when wanderer Mark Fowler returned home and confessed to his girlfriend Diane Butcher that he was HIV positive.

Diane encouraged Mark to go for counselling, saying that she would go with him. But Mark found it difficult to respond and blamed his gay counsellor Steve for spreading the virus. Mark's only comforts were Diane's kindness and patience, and a six-pack of beer.

In June 1991, his old girlfriend from Newcastle, Gill Robinson, came looking for him, thinking that they could support each other through their illness. But Mark, angry at the world and not wanting any reminders of his infection around, denied he was HIV positive to Gill. He had thought he'd contracted the virus from her, but when she revealed it was the other way round his guilt only made him drink more.

Diane persuaded him that booze would only help the virus to develop, and realising that Diane truly cared for him, he suggested that they marry. Diane knew that she was out of her depth and couldn't help Mark anymore and gently turned him down. But there was already another woman waiting in the wings for Mark – his sister's landlady, Rachel Kominski.

Mark and Rachel ended up in bed together before he told her that he was HIV positive, but her concern for him overran her anger at his deception and when she tested negative for the virus, Mark was forgiven for his omission.

Rachel persuaded Mark that he had to tell his parents, and on Christmas Day 1991 he broke the news, 'I've got this virus . . .' But Pauline and Arthur weren't just shocked, they were ignorant and their ignorance was a barrier to communication.

They resented Rachel's 'interference', thinking that discussion should be restricted to 'family'. Pauline told her son that she still loved him but Arthur remained distant, and it soon became obvious that he didn't understand about the virus. He didn't want Mark seeing Martin – he even refused to dig his allotment with a spade Mark had touched. Mark tried to break down the barriers by giving his parents leaflets about AIDS and HIV, and eventually they were both made to understand that none of the family was at risk.

After he split from Rachel (she became frustrated at his inability to open up and trust her) Mark went looking for Gill, because he knew that she would understand how he felt. When he tracked her down he was confronted with a vision of his own future – Gill had already developed AIDS.

The former lovers obviously still cared for each other very much, and Mark offered to take care of her. Reluctantly she accepted and he moved into her pokey flat and slept on the floor. Gill was tormented with splitting headaches and was visibly getting weaker by the day. So Mark decided to move her to the Square where he could keep an eye on her. She would require full-time nursing, and so Mark gave up his motorcycle-couriering job to take care of her. But the lack of income meant they couldn't afford to pay rent, and so they moved into the squat at number 23 above Sam and Ricky.

As they spent more time with each other, Mark and Gill rekindled their love, and Mark decided to make Gill's final days as happy as possible and made secret plans to marry her.

Gill soon became so frail that she had to be moved into a hospice where she could die with painless dignity. One day in June, Mark announced that he was taking her out for the day – to the registrar's office where they were married!

But the excitement of the wedding day had been too much for Gill, and Mark called for an ambulance to take her from the honeymoon suite back to the hospice. And the next day he watched his wife die.

This experience again made Mark turn to drink, but in time he came to terms with Gill's death and his own mortality to become the sanest and most reasonable voice in Albert Square.

Mark's infection tormented him again when he fell for his sister's flatmate Shelley Lewis. It was on a weekend trip to Amsterdam that they finally fell into each other's arms, but when Mark backed off at the last minute, Shelley demanded an explanation.

What she heard confused and angered her, and they returned to Walford separately and ignored each other for weeks before they were brought together for a Christmas reunion. Ironically, it was Mandy who slyly engineered their tryst: it turned out she had guessed that Mark was HIV years before when she had mischievously read Gill's diary. As Mark had been a good friend to her, she did a little bit of festive matchmaking and put Shelley straight on a few points. It was the best Christmas present Mark had ever had.

DRUGS

Marijuana, heroin, Ecstasy. All these drugs have been experimented with in Albert Square, but instead of getting the residents high, they've created heartache and misery.

When Mark and his friend Owen let eleven-year-old Cassie Carpenter puff on their joint in 1986, the Carpenters wouldn't speak to the Fowlers for weeks. Mark was a regular user and his joint smoking led to experimentation with heroin which was supplied by addict Nick Cotton.

Nick had developed an addiction while he was a teenager, but had kicked the habit at various times in his life. However, he always returned to the drug, and stole and cheated to pay for his fixes.

His mum made a final desperate bid to wean her son of the drug in 1991 when she locked him in his room and forced him to go cold turkey. Although Nick did beat his addiction, it wasn't the last time drugs were used in *EastEnders*.

In 1992 aspiring footballer Aidan Brosnan took Ecstasy at a rave with his girlfriend Mandy Salter and mate Ricky Butcher. Aidan had hoped the drug would lift his spirits and take his mind off the knee injury that had put paid to his footballing career. But by a freak of nature, Aidan became the exception that proved the rule that drugs are dangerous – he had an allergic reaction to the pill – enhanced by painkillers for his injury – and ended up in hospital.

Shelley Lewis's dope smoking had a slightly less serious side effect – the wrath of her flatmate, Michelle Fowler. Michelle caught Shelley and her college friends Clem and Russell smoking a joint when they should have been babysitting Vicki. However, on a future trip to Amsterdam, even holier-than-thou Michelle had to admit that there was indeed pleasure in the occasional toke when she puffed and spluttered her way through her first-ever joint.

She was less than pleased, however, when Clem let her unwittingly carry hash through customs. Clem couldn't see the problem – after all, she hadn't been caught – but Michelle flushed his stash down the toilet.

DRUNKENNESS

Angie Watts was *EastEnders*' celebrated drunk, and like some of her neighbours, she too had her driving licence taken away for driving under the influence. Angie was caught over the limit on the way back from a ladies' darts team match. Pete Beale also tipped the breathalyser after he smashed Mehmet's car in 1989 and had his licence taken away.

But by far and away *EastEnders*' most memorable incident of drunk driving was at Christmas 1992, when Pat knocked down and killed Stephanie Watson. She was sentenced to six months in jail after being convicted for the crime.

Thankfully though, most of Albert Square's drinkers don't get behind the wheel when they've had a few – they sit in their living rooms and mope.

Mark Fowler drank heavily for a while as he came to terms with his infection with HIV and the death of his wife. Ricky Butcher took to the bottle after his wife Sam left him in 1992, but he soon realised that booze was not the answer.

In fact the only one to realise that alcohol doesn't solve any situation was Angie herself. She spent several months 'dry' when she started managing the Dagmar, but her frustration at her attempts to win back Den soon led her straight to the gin bottle.

But most of the drinking in *EastEnders* is confined to a sociable tipple in the Queen Vic. Occasionally the guv'nor has to chuck out a few depressed and sodden souls at closing, but mostly folk in Albert Square know how to hold their liquor.

GAYS

The East End was traditionally a mecca for gays. Drag bars opened up near the docks for the sailors on shore overnight, and in the melting pot of the East End of London, homosexuality became just another facet of life.

But in Albert Square, gay men and women are conspicuous by their absence. Only two of Walford's long-term inhabitants have been gay, and they were Colin Russell and Barry Clark, an odd couple who lived at number 3.

Colin was in his late thirties and Barry was only twenty when he moved into the flat. But as Colin was so law-abiding, the two men waited until Barry was 21 (the homosexual age of consent) before going to bed with each other. It was an unusual relationship; Barry sponged off the affluent Colin who seemed to get little in return from his boyfriend. The couple endured 'friendly' jibes from the likes of Pete Beale, and the ignorance of the likes of Dot who nearly fainted when she washed their bed linen in the launderette and realised they shared a bed!

Eventually the gentleman and the lad realised they were incompatible and split up.

Colin later dated Guido Smith, but it was obvious he was still carrying a torch for Barry. Guido took it upon himself to tell Barry this before Colin left the Square to live with his brother in Bristol in February 1989. The two men declared their friendship for each other and kissed goodbye any feelings of anger or disappointment.

Other gay men who have made an appearance in Walford were friends of Mark he met at the AIDS drop-in centre. First there was his counsellor Steve, and then his friend Joe Wallace, who worked as Ian's chef for a while. When Mark's wife Gill was in the hospice she was looked after by a gay carer, George.

So far, the only lesbian to make it to Albert Square was a social-worker friend of Dr Legg's, who joined him for a drink in the Vic once. But it can't be long before another gay person finds a home in Albert Square.

RACISM

By and large, people of all creeds, colours, and persuasions are allowed to live their lives how they wish in Walford, the local motto being 'live and let live'. But a few East End locals can't help themselves from thinking that Walford would be a better place if 'those foreigners' weren't around.

Nick Cotton is guilty of holding the most right-wing views, seeing dark skin as a legitimate reason to torment a person. His mum, Dot, didn't take kindly to blacks and Asians (or gays) either, until she came to call Jules Tavernier a friend.

So when Naima Jeffrey's shop was daubed in racist graffiti, Nick Cotton was the number one suspect. Although it was never proved that he was the culprit, everyone knew he was capable of the crime. Naima's successors, Ashraf and Sufia Karim, also had neo-Nazi slogans painted on the shop. They were also the victims of racism at home – their house in Victoria Road had had a brick thrown through a window.

During a spate of burglaries in the area in 1986, the police suspected Kelvin Carpenter – solely because he was black. And when Nick Cotton told the coppers that he had seen Clyde Tavernier next to Eddie Royle's body, they were only too ready to believe that the murder had been committed by a black man. Indeed, most of the Square was ready to condemn Clyde; only his white girlfriend Michelle Fowler stood by him and was willing to go on the run with him to avoid arrest.

Clyde and Michelle's romance wasn't *EastEnders*' first interracial relationship. Ricky Butcher dated Shireen Karim as often as her dad would allow, and health visitor Carmel Roberts married her white boyfriend Matthew Jackson. And of course Walford's own Sue Osman married Turkish Ali and bravely coped with his interfering family.

Most recently the Jacksons have proved yet again that race is no barrier to love, with Alan even taking on Carol's wayward brood – now that's really love!

THE QUEEN VICTORIA PUB

The Queen Vic is *EastEnders*' centrepiece, the jewel in its crown. It presents us with two dramas simultaneously: those of a public house and a private home. It's a case of Upstairs Downstairs, and no matter what happens on the first floor, the punters in the bar must never know a thing.

The Vic was built in the 1880s and originally it had two bars – the Public and the Saloon. However, in 1985, the publican at the time, Den Watts, decided to dismantle the partition between the bars. But Den's legacy to the Vic is far greater than structural.

Den and his wife Angie made the grotty East End boozer seem more like a music hall with their farcical fights and melodrama. The warring Wattses stamped their unique mark on the pub and made it a second home to everyone who came and went in Albert Square. East End regulars either pop in for a swift half at lunchtime or a knees-up of an evening.

If you're ever feeling lonely you can be sure to find a friend in the Queen Vic. And if you're in need of a few extra pennies, you could probably do a couple of shifts for the guv'nors. Over the years many of the East Enders have pulled a pint of Churchill's in the Queen Vic: Kathy, Pauline, Wicksy, Lofty, Sharon, Donna, Michelle, Clyde, Shelley, Pat, Frank, Mo, Tracy from the flower stall, Grant, Phil, Eddie, Jan, and of course Den and Angie, have all done their best – and worst – to keep the customers satisfied.

And Pauline, Dot, Pat, Mary and Ethel have all had a stint with the Pledge and duster doing the cleaning.

The Vic has played host to tears, traumas and triumphs. It's where the East Enders congregate for a fight, a party or a gossip – the Queen Vic is the heart of Albert Square, pumping tittle-tattle round the houses quicker than lightning.

The Vic's crown was challenged in 1987 when Luxford and Copley's former area manager, James Willmott-Brown, defected to rival brewers Gladstones and re-opened the Dagmar in Turpin Road. With Angie serving cocktails round the corner, everyone expected the drama in the Vic to stop. But the old dame didn't disappoint, and still attracted the best entertainment *EastEnders* had to offer. Tom died suddenly in the gents; Cindy became the second woman to conceive after just one night of passion in the bar (the first was Michelle); and Den's substitute attraction of a video jukebox enticed local drug dealers to the pub.

It also drove the regulars away, so Den wriggled out of his agreement with the jukebox firm, and the locals soon wandered back through the famous swing doors. Pete's perennial pewter tankard was taken down from the top shelf, and once again the Vic became a friendly East End local. Den also tried to keep his customers by offering some decent grub at lunchtime. In fact food has often caused as many fights in the Vic as the booze and women!

Time was when all you could get for your lunch in the Queen Vic was a roll supplied by Sue (and which you could have for half the price over the road in the café). When Ian finished college he encouraged Den to install a hot-food counter, but Ian's culinary skills weren't enhanced by Pat serving the nosh while she still had a fag in her mouth!

When Ian left, the lunchtime trade dropped off: unsurprisingly people weren't impressed by a half reheated baked potato and rock-solid baked beans. (When the recession – and Tricky Dicky's meddling – led to the demise of Ian's Meal Machine, he once again got the contract for lunches in the pub. Sharon was impressed by the food, but not by the conduct of Cindy and Hattie feuding while they served.)

When the Firm made Dennis an offer he couldn't refuse

in 1988, he stepped down as the Vic's landlord and new guv'nors Frank and Pat moved in. Things were different during their reign: there was plenty of friction but few sparks. Most of the trouble happened upstairs as Pat adapted to being a stepmum, and Mo tried to come to terms with no longer being the most important woman in Frank's life. Although they ran a tight ship, Frank and Pat couldn't steer it through such interesting waters as the Wattses had. So when they made the decision to leave the tenancy themselves in 1990 because they were over-stretching themselves (they also ran the B&B and the car lot), the news didn't make many ripples.

Sharon saw this as her perfect opportunity to claim the Vic for herself. Uncrowned as the 'Princess Victoria', Sharon felt that the pub that had been her home since she could remember and was hers by right. So she and her boyfriend Wicksy applied for the tenancy, certain that the Queen Vic was theirs.

They were obviously very shocked when they learnt that outsider – and worse, former copper – Eddie Royle had won the tenancy. Eddie had retired early from the force because he'd despised the way the rules were bent and broken by his colleagues. He took on the Vic with a view to it sustaining him till he died.

But not only would his days as Queen Vic publican be numbered, but his few months in the job were packed with drama. He first caused a stir when he made a play for Kathy Beale, who was flattered but politely turned him down. When the lonely Eddie offered himself to Sharon after she confided her hard times with Grant, it wasn't long before Grant's fist was pulverising Eddie's face.

Eddie's indiscretion had tripped a wire in Grant, who let loose on the unprepared guv'nor, and Eddie ended up in hospital. It took Eddie a long time to recover from the beating and for months he hid upstairs while chaos ruled behind the bar.

His year as landlord of East London's most famous pub came to an end when he was stabbed to death in

September 1991. The pub was closed for a while, and as the locals absorbed the shock of the brutal killing, Sharon prepared her assault on the tenancy.

Finally in October 1991, she was granted a temporary licence to reopen the pub. But to get the licence permanently she was going to have to come up with some cash. So when Grant begged her to marry him at Christmas, Sharon agreed to the nuptials on the grounds that he secure the Vic for her. And with the help of his brother Phil, that's exactly what Grant did. It was with pride and love that he presented his wife with the licensee sign to go above the door. But what Grant didn't realise was that Sharon actually loved the Vic more than she loved him.

He grew tired of playing second fiddle to a boozer and took to drinking with his mates until all hours. Sharon responded by starting an inevitable affair with his brother Phil. Although the affair petered out and Sharon returned to her husband, the suspense of Grant ever finding out about the betrayal can still send a chill down the spine.

Perhaps the most significant event in the Queen Vic's history was the fire on 27 October 1992, which was started by Grant as an insurance fiddle. Not only did it cause so much damage that the site was almost declared unsafe, but when the inferno was at its worst, Sharon was trapped upstairs.

She was rescued by the emergency services and taken to hospital suffering from smoke inhalation. When she was released, she moved back into the smoke-charred building and set about a refurbishment. For weeks the glory of the Queen Vic was shrouded in green netting while the builders and decorators completed a stunning transformation. The pub reopened on 24 November, and Sharon had done her mum proud. Gone was the yellowing paintwork and the dingy corners, and in their place were upholstered seats and a cosy atmosphere. Sharon had taken the gem and given it a good polish, and the Vic was all the better for it.

However, she couldn't give her marriage a lick of paint and things deteriorated even further between her and

Grant. At one point he was so sure that she had another fella that he followed her to a gig at Michelle's college expecting to find her in bed with someone. (In fact, it was Michelle's boyfriend Clyde who was being cheated on – the two men caught Michelle red-handed and red-faced having a one-night stand.)

Even though Sharon denied cheating on her husband, Grant was still so hurt by her behaviour that he confessed he'd torched her precious pub because he'd needed the insurance money to pay a gangster. Sharon was hurt beyond measure – not only had he nearly killed her (even if it was accidental) but her husband had wilfully ruined the most important thing in her life.

In the end her unspoken guilt at sleeping with his brother led to a truce, but Sharon will do her damnedest to make sure Grant never twigs about the affair, because that would definitely mean losing the Vic. Following Roly's death in October 1993, the pub was all she had left of her childhood, meaning she would fight for the Vic even more ferociously than ever.

Sharon is maintaining the standards that her parents set, always serving the customers with a smile and making sure Grant heavies any louts outside. Sharon reigns supreme behind the bar; perhaps more than any other East Ender she has her own turf, her patch. And as long as she doesn't turn to the gin like her mum, she'll be protecting her baby for years to come.

TRAGEDY AND TRAUMA

Albert Square has been the scene of more melodrama than the old East End music halls ever knew. Confessions, confrontations and calamity have all found an audience in Walford, and the players in these show pieces have been our friends, the East Enders.

Emotions run high in their neck of the woods, and on a few occasions feelings have spun out of control to create some complex and dramatic situations. Lives are changed forever by these events, which are inscribed on the hearts of the East Enders like carvings in stone . . .

MICHELLE TELLS DEN SHE'S PREGNANT, OCTOBER 1985 – SEE 'MICHELLE AND SHARON' AND 'ADULTERY'

ANGIE'S OVERDOSE, FEBRUARY 1986 – SEE 'DEN AND ANGIE'

ANGIE TELLS DEN SHE'S DYING, OCTOBER 1986

When Angie Watts got up early on the morning of 16 October 1986, she had a hangover. As usual. And as usual her husband Dennis was prowling the Queen Vic pub like a predatory lion, and it was clear he had something on his mind. What Angie couldn't have known, though, was that the next half-hour would be the most harrowing she had ever known.

She got up to face the day without her protective layer of make-up to find Den giving the window cleaner a bucket of hot water so he could get on with his job. Before breakfast, Den relieved himself of the weight on his mind and told Angie that he wanted a divorce.

Angie tried hard not to let the anger and hurt show on her face – maybe this was just another of Den's mind games – and so she went upstairs to put the kettle on. Den followed her, keen to make sure she understood him properly, but their intimacy was invaded by the window cleaner who needed fresh supplies for his bucket.

The window cleaner was to interrupt them many times that morning, innocent to the anguish of the Wattses. As Den busied himself with Roly's needs, Angie put her warpaint on. She studied herself carefully in the mirror and meticulously applied the mask that could hide her pain. It also shrouded her cunning mind which was hatching an amazing scam.

Den should have known better than to think that Angie would give up on the marriage so easily, but even an old hand like him couldn't have predicted the lengths Angie was prepared to go to to save their union.

In a quiet moment she told Den that he couldn't divorce her because Sharon would never forgive him. She said she only had six months to live (all the boozing had damaged her liver), and that if he could just stick it out for a few more months, Sharon would be spared the pain of a split and he'd be free to marry Jan anyway.

Den was wary of her words. He said he'd been to see Dr Legg about her and the doctor hadn't mentioned a terminal illness. 'Well he wouldn't, would he?' she replied.

So Den was forced to give his marriage another go, even though he wasn't entirely convinced of Angie's illness. Unsure, he promised to make Angie's last few months worth living – they would have a second honeymoon, call a truce and give happiness their best shot.

Angie herself couldn't quite believe the stunt she'd pulled, so when Den issued the warning 'If I ever find out you're lying . . . I'll kill you', Angie knew that her days as Albert Square's greatest storyteller had only just begun.

ARTHUR HAS A BREAKDOWN, DECEMBER 1986

While his wife was in the Vic on Christmas Day 1986 putting two and two together about Michelle and Den, Arthur was left babysitting Martin and Vicki at number 45.

He had been snappy and preoccupied for months, but no one in Albert Square had predicted that he was heading for a breakdown. But that's exactly what happened.

Brooding in the living room as the kids were upstairs asleep, the pressure finally got to him, and in a fit of desperation, Arthur stood up and swept the teapot off the table and proceeded to demolish the Fowlers' living room.

The stresses of recent years – his long-term unemployment, the unplanned arrivals of Martin and Vicki, and the responsibility of paying for Michelle's wedding that never was – had finally taken their toll.

The final straw had been his arrest for stealing the Christmas Club money. All he had wanted to do was to give his only daughter the sort of wedding every father wants to give, and the fact that the wedding had ended without a marriage only underlined the futility of what he'd done.

Arthur had started the Christmas Club early in the year so his neighbours could put a little away each week and get a lump sum back for Christmas. Every week, he dutifully collected their money and deposited it in the building society.

In the summer, when Lofty and Michelle announced their imminent nuptials, Arthur panicked about how to pay for the event. The only source of money available to him was the Christmas Club fund, and so he withdrew the money to give Michelle what he hoped would be the best day of her life.

He intended to pay the members of the Christmas Club back with the insurance from a robbery he would commit himself. On 6 November, he made a point of telling the whole of Walford that he'd withdrawn the money and that they could collect their savings. That night, while everyone was in the pub, he faked a break-in which was only 'discovered' when Pauline returned home from the Vic.

She sussed immediately what Arthur had done and then realised where he'd gotten the money to pay for the wedding. And it wasn't long before the police also realised that Arthur was the instigator of the burglary. After a moment's resistance, he confessed to the crime and helped the police all he could.

He was ashamed and racked with guilt, and his shame only increased as Christmas drew close. His neighbours taunted him with tales of how they didn't have their money to pay for Christmas presents, and Arthur became distant and irritable. So when news of his breakdown got out, sympathy was hard to find.

Pauline hoped her husband's depression was temporary, but when he didn't even flinch when a cup of boiling water was accidentally spilt over him, she knew he needed professional help.

He was admitted into hospital where Pauline visited him frequently. The visits were unsettling for her as Arthur rocked rhythmically in his chair talking nonsense. When she told him not to worry – 'after all, life's not a bowl of cherries, is it love?' – Arthur replied: 'Cherries only get eaten anyway.'

When Arthur finally came home from the hospital in March, he was a changed man. Rehabilitated through therapy, he was determined to get a job and make his family proud of him again. Instead of being depressed he was full of the joys of life, always looking for the silver lining. He was convicted for the robbery and sentenced to 28 days in prison, and when he was released he felt like he had served his penance and set about paying everyone back every single penny he had taken.

WILLMOTT-BROWN RAPES KATHY, JULY 1988

She thought it could never happen to her again, but Kathy's worst nightmare reared its ugly head for the second time when she was raped by James Wilmott-Brown on 7 July 1988.

She had been working behind the bar in his pub, the Dagmar, for a while and even though he had made advances she still stayed to spite her husband, Pete.

Pete had accused Kath of having an affair with Collis-Brown, as some of the locals 'affectionately' called him. But Kathy had always politely turned him down and she was determined to prove that to Pete.

Towards the end of 1987, it seemed that Willmott-Brown had gotten the message and was now offering Kathy nothing more than friendship while her marriage paddled through turbulent waters. So when he invited her for an after-hours drink in the flat above the pub, Kathy accepted. Willmott-Brown took this as consent and attempted to kiss her. Kath fought him off, telling him that this wasn't what she wanted at all, but he persisted and, wrestling her to the floor, forced himself upon her.

It was Den who found her a few hours later, a devastated and destroyed woman, sobbing uncontrollably. 'I want to pull my skin off,' she told him. 'I want to die. I really want to die.'

Den took her round to Pauline and Arthur's for comfort while he made plans to seek his own brand of East End retribution. In the wee small hours of the morning, the Dagmar was set on fire, and as the flames lit up the East End sky Den was seen gloating.

Willmott-Brown meanwhile had been arrested and charged. He was bailed and a few months later returned to the Square to bribe Kath into dropping the charges. Somehow, she found the strength to fight him, and actually tricked him into confessing the bribe within police earshot.

This, and Kathy's brave and emotional testimony, was enough to convict the yuppie and he was sentenced to three years' imprisonment.

MICHELLE TELLS SHARON ABOUT DEN, APRIL 1989

Following Den's mysterious disappearance in February 1989, the police reached the conclusion that he was almost certainly dead, and in March they informed a tearful Sharon of their suspicions.

She was so upset by the news – Den had always seemed so invincible – that Michelle thought it would be of comfort to her best friend to know that Den lived on in Vicki.

At the time, the two friends shared a flat at number 43, and one night in April Michelle used the privacy of their home to drop her bombshell on Sharon.

Michelle wondered if perhaps Sharon had already guessed, but like many women who suspect their husbands of affairs, chosen to ignore it rather than confront it. But Sharon didn't have a clue – why would she? – and had no idea of what Michelle was planning. Michelle had gone out to First Til Last and bought the essential ingredients to a girls' night in. She returned to the flat, and while she prepared some food encouraged her pal to talk about the past.

Naturally, it wasn't long before their talk turned to Den – after all, each of them had worshipped him in her own way. Michelle tried to comfort Sharon by telling her that Den would never be dead as long as people remembered him. But Sharon could sense that Michelle meant something more than that.

Sharon sat puzzled in the living room as Michelle created in the kitchen. 'What exactly do you mean?' Sharon asked.

'Don't you know?' was the reply.

Sharon looked blank and shook her head, and so with her heart in her mouth Michelle just stated the fact: 'Den's Vicki's father.'

Sharon's initial reaction was disbelief, but then when it became clear that Michelle wasn't joking, Sharon had never felt more hurt in her whole life.

The two people whom she had loved the most had let her down the most. She felt awkward – her father and her best friend? How could they? How could they do that to her?

She asked a few inane questions, but they were both too shellshocked for anything either said to make much sense. Then suddenly, in something close to rage, Sharon just collected a few things together and stormed out.

Michelle followed her, pleading with her: 'Sharon, we have to talk.' But Sharon was having none of it. Scared, and unsure of everything she had thought she could believe, she ran off into the night, giving no indication of where she was going.

It was Wicksy who finally revealed where Sharon was, but it wasn't until Vicki's life was threatened by meningitis that Sharon could bring herself to talk to Michelle at Vicki's bedside in hospital. But once the air was cleared, they became closer than they had ever been before.

CINDY TELLS IAN THE TRUTH ABOUT WICKSY,
AUGUST 1990 – SEE 'WEDDINGS'

KATHY'S SHOWDOWN WITH WILLMOTT-BROWN,
JANUARY 1992

The first hint that Kathy's nemesis was returning to Walford came when Ian was outbid at an auction for the pizza parlour by a mysterious telephone bidder called 'Brown'.

Mr Brown had also purchased one of the flats at number

43, but it wasn't until later that the locals found out Mr Brown's true identity.

It came like a thunderbolt to the heart when the Beales found out Willmott-Brown had returned – as far as they were concerned he still had another two years to serve in jail.

But the toff had been let out for good behaviour after just a year, and intended on returning to the Square to rebuild his reputation – and make Kathy his wife!

In prison, he had convinced himself that Kathy really did love him and that she had only prosecuted him so that Pete would not have accused her of having an affair. He told himself that he hadn't raped Kathy – he had made love to her – and he deluded himself that he could convince the East Enders of this too.

When Ian and Pete discovered his festering presence in the Square, they tried to tell Kath before she found out for herself. But they were too late. Willmott-Brown had tracked her down and said 'Hello' with a smile that made her heart freeze.

Everyone in Walford begged him to leave, but James thought he had some power over Kathy that would make her come clean about their 'undying love'.

She was brave and went to confront him, but his kids, Luke and Sophie, were there and she couldn't say in front of their innocent ears the words of hatred she was desperate to speak.

Pete, as ever, was less conciliatory and decided words would never get through to James – and they would certainly never hurt him as much as he had hurt Kathy – and so he arranged a good ol' East End lynch mob. Surely an ex-army man would understand a well-executed bit of violence?

Kath, meanwhile, had turned to her level-headed friend Rachel for support, and the two women arranged to meet James at a hotel for a talk. But the brash arrival of a vengeful Pete – who had vowed to protect his estranged wife – put paid to the gentle approach. And the heavy approach (the mob setting upon Willmott-Brown in a car park) only made the yuppie more determined to make a go of life in Albert Square.

And for a week or so it looked like he might defy the wishes of his neighbours and stay put. Kath knew it was down to her to make him leave – after all, she was the only person he would listen to.

Pete offered to accompany her as she went for her showdown with the man who had raped her. Kath accepted – it felt normal for her husband (even if they were separated) to be there – and in many ways, James had hurt Pete just as much.

When James saw Kathy at his door, he was delighted. He thought she had finally come to her senses and realised that they were perfect for each other. But when he noticed Pete standing behind her, James knew that Kath was not there to proclaim her love.

The three of them, locked inside his house, with his unpacked tea chests all over the place, had unexpectedly invited themselves to a party where they would play the game of Truth.

And the truth hurt. As James declared his love for Kath, his delusions became obvious, so Kath shattered his dreams telling him that he wasn't even worth getting upset about any more – that was only letting him win.

'It was just sex,' she said. 'Hateful sex.' She didn't want to use the word 'rape' because that made it too important, and she wanted him to know that everything about him was worthless.

After she had said her piece she locked herself in the bathroom to fix her badly run mascara, giving Pete the opportunity to put the boot in.

Kathy's bravery and Pete's threats were enough for the smarmy toff to repack the few possessions he had unpacked, and that was the last Albert Square saw of James Willmott-Brown. Hopefully.

Following the fire at the Vic, Michelle Fowler decided that what her best friend Sharon needed was a good night out, away from Albert Square and the marital mire she was wallowing in with Grant.

There was a band playing at her student union bar at the Polytechnic of Greater London, and so she dragged Sharon along for a night's distraction.

Sharon knew she would feel pretty out of place with a bunch of students, and she needed plenty of convincing that her brash pink mini-skirt suit wasn't over the top. It was, but Michelle knew that wasn't the point; as long as Sharon dressed as herself she would relax.

As it turned out, everyone else was wearing jeans like Michelle, and Sharon – a pretty blonde woman in a short skirt – stood out like a flamingo in a sea of pigeons, and attracted much male attention.

As Sharon fended them off left, right and centre (they were also interested in the bottle of vodka she'd brought from the Vic), Michelle was saddled with a naive student who seemed overly interested in her.

Meanwhile, back at the ranch, Grant was becoming ever more sure that Sharon had another man, and he persuaded Michelle's boyfriend Clyde to go to the college with him for a showdown with their errant women.

They jumped over a wall to avoid the college security men, and tracked the girls down to a room in the halls of residence. Grant was sure that Sharon – who was by now very drunk – would be flirting and kissing another man, and he was determined to catch her in the act.

So together Grant and Clyde kicked in the door, and sure enough there was a naked girlfriend in bed with a stranger. But it was the wrong girlfriend – it was Michelle!

Clyde was hurt and angry and he lashed out at the guy – a twenty-year-old student called Jack Woodman – as he tried to keep himself decent with a duvet.

Grant left Michelle and Clyde to it and stormed off to

find Sharon, and when he found her in a communal room downstairs, he was quick to accuse the boy she was talking to of sleeping with his wife.

It was Michelle's college friend Shelley who defended Sharon, but Grant still asked her if there was anybody else.

As Sharon stared her husband in the eye, her heart beat like a hammer as she weighed up the pros and cons of telling him about Phil. God knows, Grant deserved to be told after the way he had behaved, but just as she was about to confess her sin, Sharon said a soft no, which made her heart stand still.

Grant was more willing to confess his crime, and out of spite he told her that he had been the one who'd set fire to her precious Vic. Sharon could never forgive him – he had ruined the single most important thing in her life, and been responsible for almost killing her. She offered words of contempt and retribution, and she told him their marriage was over.

Michelle and Clyde's relationship was also over, and the two friends left the college grounds that night arm in arm, promising in jest that 'we must do this more often!'

PAT'S DRINK DRIVING, DECEMBER 1992

It was Christmas Eve, and Pat Butcher had just knocked off work for a festive G&T in the Vic. Work for Pat was running her own successful cab firm, PatCabs, and because it was Christmas she had all her drivers out taking people to seasonal reunions.

So when a regular customer needed a last-minute ride, Pat felt she had no option but to take him herself. Her friends in the pub told her to forget it – it was Christmas – and stay and have another drink. But Pat decided she couldn't let her customer down, and set off for the quick journey.

As she neared her pick-up in a quiet suburban street,

somebody ran out in front of a car coming from nowhere like a ghost. Pat slammed on the brakes, but it was too late – she had already knocked down the pedestrian.

The adrenalin passed through her like electricity and she sat frozen at the wheel of her car. Eventually the emergency services arrived and the pedestrian – a 22-year-old girl called Stephanie Watson – was taken to hospital. As a matter of procedure, Pat was breathalysed. She was stunned when she was told she was over the blood alcohol limit.

Pat was escorted back to the Square the following morning – Christmas Day – where none of her family was in the mood for celebrating as they had just heard that her mother-in-law, Mo, had died.

Pat was restless and insisted on visiting the hospital where Stephanie was being cared for, only to be told that her worst fears had come true – Stephanie had died.

Pat blamed herself entirely and was inconsolable. She didn't want to leave the house, she certainly didn't want to get in a car ever again. And all Frank's gentle persuasion couldn't help – Pat just wanted to be left alone to feel guilty.

In February she had a hearing where a date was set for her trial. In the public gallery was Stephanie's mother. Mrs Watson made a note of Pat's address and later paid her a visit. Pat welcomed her, but Mrs Watson had not come for a cup of tea. She meant to tell Pat just what she had taken from her. Stephanie had been her only daughter, who had been engaged to be married. She had been the apple of her eye and now Mrs Watson didn't know what she was living for.

Pat explained that her life had been upturned too, but Mrs Watson could find no forgiveness and told Pat she would have to live with her contempt forever. So when Pat was eventually sentenced to six months in jail, she felt she deserved more. But her own unforgiving conscience was punishment enough.

When Michelle Fowler had a one-night stand with fellow student Jack Woodman, she could not have known that a moment's passion would lead to such unbearable pain.

Jack fell in love with her, and her dismissal of him as just a mistake made him obsessive about her. He turned up at her parents' house on Christmas Day to give her a single red rose. Then he started taking photos in the market and worming his way into the affections of Michelle's friends and family. For a while, no one could understand why she thought he was 'creepy', but when he started making unsettling phone calls the East Enders realised Jack was a problem.

But when Michelle went to collect Vicki from primary school on 4 March and found her little girl was missing, she never thought that Jack was mad enough to have kidnapped her.

At first Michelle blamed herself for being late, and as she checked with Vicki's teachers the guilt was eating her up. After she had made sure Vicki had definitely left the school grounds, she returned to Albert Square to see if one of the other mothers had brought her home.

They hadn't, so Michelle started phoning everyone she knew, but no one had seen anything, and Michelle was forced to call the police.

The law took it all very seriously. A specially trained WPC was drafted in to take care of Michelle's needs and questions, while a sensitive inspector led the hunt to find Vicki.

Pauline and Sharon (who had just returned from a holiday in Florida) took turns to wait with 'Chelle. The police had to be sure that no one Michelle knew might have taken Vicki out of spite, and she had to endure personal questions about Lofty and Den. Then, in a flash, it came to her that Jack might just be mad enough to have pulled a stunt like this, and within an hour the police were lying in wait for him outside the college halls of residence.

As Jack cycled into view it was obvious he didn't have

Vicki with him. Nevertheless, he was still subjected to a gruelling interrogation which forced him into displaying his traits of madness. He had a convincing alibi, but the inspector didn't trust Jack and ordered him to be kept under watch.

Vicki was not the only member of the Fowler clan who was missing – Arthur was nowhere to be seen as well. He returned late from a clandestine meeting with his mistress, Christine Hewitt, to find his family in turmoil, and his guilt over his affair intensified.

The Square rallied round, with the men organising search parties for the little girl. When they found a jacket that looked a lot like Vicki's they feared the worst had happened, but thankfully the garment belonged to someone else.

The next morning, Vicki's picture was on the front pages of national newspapers in the hope that someone might see her and recognise her. Back in Albert Square, Sharon and Michelle waited together looking through photo albums and talking about Den.

The breakthrough came when a cashier in a toyshop recognised Vicki from her picture in the paper when she came in with a middle-aged woman who was buying her toys.

The canny cashier started asking questions like, 'How old are you?' The woman answered, 'Five', but Vicki insisted she was six. After they left the shop, the cashier phoned the police who came round and checked the name on the cheque that the woman had written. Mrs A. Whittingham. They ran it through the computer and found an address for Mrs Whittingham, and then positioned a police car outside her home in the hope that she would have Vicki with her.

Michelle insisted on going, even though the police thought it might be better if Pauline went in case it was a false alarm. But it wasn't.

As Audrey Whittingham came home from the shops with a small girl in tow, she fumbled with her keys. And in those few moments the little girl wearing a red-hooded jacket turned round and Michelle could see that it was Vicki.

Mother and daughter were reunited but the nightmare wasn't over. Although Vicki seemed untroubled by her nights away from her mum, Michelle tortured herself for weeks, unable to forgive herself for being just a couple of minutes late.

WAIFS AND STRAYS

Over the years Albert Square has taken in many a lonely heart. People with nowhere else to go have ended up in Walford penniless, scared and angry.

In a community where families are so important, these friendless souls stick out like a painfully sore thumb. They come to Albert Square trying to make some sense out of their screwed-up lives, and usually – for a little while – they find some support and some serenity, but almost always they leave as unsettled and insecure as they ever were.

MARY SMITH

With her baby daughter Annie tucked under her arm, Mary moved to the Square on 5 March 1985. The council had found her a bedsit at number 23, and she was grateful for her new home – until she was told that Reg Cox had died there.

Mary's real name was Theresa, and she had run away from her devout Catholic family in Stockport to get away from her mother's meddling. Her severe make-up, back-combed hair and aggressive clothes were a barrier to making friends in Albert Square, but baby Annie made sure people kept an eye out for her.

Mary's downstairs neighbours were Sue and Ali Osman. After the accusations that they hadn't been good enough neighbours to notice Reg was missing, Sue was keen to make sure the fingers wouldn't point at her a second time and so she 'looked in' on Mary to the point of interfering. Sue often offered to babysit for Mary – she practically insisted following the death of her own son, Hassan – but Mary never seemed to show any thanks.

She mistrusted everyone, convinced that the world was against her. The truth is the friendly Walfordians gave Mary several chances to get on her feet, but she bit their heads off at the slightest notion of patronisation or broken promises. She had a chip on her shoulder the size of her mum's Catholic conscience, and it was hard to imagine that she would ever be happy.

She didn't know much about mothering – when to get jabs, or take Annie for check-ups – but she took health visitor Carmel Roberts' advice to be criticism, thus biting the hand that could help her.

Mary was so used to her mum getting at her for any tiny fault that she found comment – criticism or not – unbearable.

Like many single parents on the 'social', Mary found it hard to make ends meet, so when her friend Sheena Mennell suggested she try stripping, Mary didn't take a lot of persuading. Sue was so pleased to know that Mary had got a job at last that she babysat without asking any difficult questions.

When Nick Cotton found out how Mary was making money, he offered her the chance to make more – by going on the game. And she did.

She was arrested for solicitation and the Square's sympathy for her rapidly diminished. Sue said she wouldn't babysit anymore as she knew it only encouraged Mary to carry on selling herself. But Mary took her action as a criticism – confirmation that the whole world was against her getting ahead.

Mary did find one ally, however – good Samaritan Andy O'Brien. She asked him to explain her court summons to her, confessing that she couldn't read or write. Andy was typically understanding and offered to teach her. Stunned by a genuine and selfless act of kindness, she misinterpreted his actions and thought he wanted something in return. When he rejected her, yet again she reacted with misplaced anger.

Dot Cotton thought it was her Christian duty to inform Mary's parents of her latest occupation, and so she phoned Mary's dad Chris. He soon arrived in the Square in his long-distance lorry ready to take Mary back with him to Stockport – if that was what she wanted. But Mary couldn't return – she hadn't told her mother Edie about Annie – and she didn't want to hear her lectures. Chris understood, but made sure Mary knew he was there if she needed him. He left her a bar of chocolate – with a twenty pound note inside the wrapper – and got back in the lorry and hit the road.

One night, when Mary had the chance of a legitimate job, she asked everyone in the Square to babysit Annie for her, but everyone refused in case she was back on the game. Desperate for cash, Mary felt she had no choice but to leave Annie alone and go out to work.

She put Annie in her cot with her favourite toys and a blanket for comfort, and she left the electric fire on so the tot wouldn't get cold, and went out to work.

A few hours later, Dot and Ethel downstairs heard Annie crying and went to investigate. When they put their ears to the door and felt that it was burning hot, they knew that there was a fire inside.

Ethel showed that she may have been old, but she certainly wasn't frail and forced the door open and rushed in to rescue Annie from the flames: she had accidentally thrown her blanket on the fire.

That was enough proof for Chris to know that Mary really couldn't cope on her own, and he returned to the Square – with Edie in tow.

It was easy to see why Mary had run away – her mum was every bit as obsessional and interfering as she'd said. And when Edie saw the smoke-charred bedsit she would hear no reason against taking Annie to live with them in Stockport.

Mary knew she would have to sort herself out – clear her debts, get a regular job and smarten up her act – if she was ever to get Annie back. The council redecorated the bedsit, and James Willmott-Brown gave her a job as the cleaner at the Dagmar.

Her boyfriend Rod Norman had to take some of the credit – he calmed her down when she was ready to fly off the handle and proved that not everybody was against her. But still her mother refused to return Annie, deciding instead to christen the child and bring her up as a Catholic. Nothing could have filled Mary with more horror – her mother's beliefs were a major reason why she'd run away all those years ago. So she went to Stockport to 'steal' her own child and bring her back. Annie was to be stolen again that Christmas, when Chris took the child with him in his lorry. But he was drunk and didn't make it out of the Square before crashing – mercifully Annie was unharmed.

Having Annie back wasn't the answer to Mary's problems, and she was still as ungrateful as ever for her neighbours' help. She started using drugs, only succeeding in alienating herself further. The drugs depressed her and made her even more irrational and, in May 1988, she took her baby and got on a bus out of Walford for good, sticking two fingers up at Albert Square – for old time's sake.

LOFTY HOLLOWAY

This loveable misfit came to Albert Square when he was thrown out of the army due to his dormant asthma. And although he got a job – and eventually a wife and kid – he never really fitted into life in the East End.

Judging by his spindly appearance (he got his nickname because of his height), it was hard to believe that George was bred for army life. But he came from a well-to-do church-going family who had been in the forces for generations. His mother had been stern and authoritarian, his father was often absent and living in barracks, so he had been shown little affection as a boy – only his auntie

Irene bestowed such love on the child (it was she who had given him his favourite toy – an old railway set).

So it was with joy and expectation that he signed up just as soon as he was old enough. The army compensated for all his faults – decisions were made for him and at last he had found somewhere where he was one of the crowd. On Civvy Street he was most definitely a misfit.

On his unwanted release, he got a job behind the bar at the Queen Vic where he put up with ridicule not just from Den, but also from the ladies' darts team who once conned him into stripping down to his boxers. (He hid in the loo out of embarrassment until Sharon gently coaxed him out.)

He never had much luck with girls. His badly cut hair, John Lennon glasses and ever-present green army jacket probably had something to do with it, but the problem with Lofty was that he just didn't understand the idea of romance. But as it turned out, he didn't need to take lessons from Valentino to end up walking down the aisle: when Michelle Fowler got pregnant, Wicksy's throwaway comment of 'who'd have her now?' got Lofty thinking.

He proposed to her well aware that she didn't love him, but he truly believed that love would grow with time. However, Michelle politely turned him down only to change her mind two months later – even though she still had reservations.

Lofty wanted to do everything right by 'Chelle. He sent flowers to the hospital when Vicki was born (these only reminded Michelle that perhaps she had made the wrong decision) and offered his £50 savings to Arthur to help pay for the wedding. These were typical Lofty gestures, but he would have done the same for a lame dog: he was so selfless that his generosity lacked emotional involvement. If Lofty helped you it was because he thought he ought to – not because he wanted to.

A tad hungover from his stag night, Lofty got up on 25 September 1986 and nervously put on his hired morning suit, ready for the church. But he complained to his best man Wicksy that he felt like a penguin and changed into his own familiar tweed jacket.

At the church his only relative was his auntie Irene. He waited and waited and eventually his bride arrived and his heart leapt. Michelle waited motionless for what seemed an eternity at the door before turning, leaving Lofty embarrassed and broken-hearted. He hid his pain well until he was alone, when he broke down and sobbed holding the box of chocolates he'd been going to share with his bride. Yet again he'd been humiliated in public, but this time it was much more than ridicule.

Most of the Square sympathised with him, making it easier for him to go about his day-to-day life. Michelle apologised and finally made his dreams come true in November when she married him in a registry office, making it clear that she wanted a provider for herself and Vicki. But that didn't matter to Lofty, because he finally had everything he wanted. For years he'd been wanting to shower his love on someone, and now his ready-made family would be the perfect recipients.

But even Lofty's enthusiasm couldn't compensate for all the obvious flaws in the marriage. He decorated his pokey flat for his wife, but only succeeded in amusing her with his taste in interior decor – dark brown paintwork and beige floral print wallpaper which would have been more at home in a rundown old people's home. Michelle made him change it – even though she was mature for her age, she was not as old as her old fogey of a husband.

When Michelle's eighteenth birthday came around, Lofty – in his kindness – wanted to make it special. He thought he might buy her a typewriter (she was on a secretarial course) or maybe something for the flat. Their friends tried to persuade him that something more intimate might be appropriate. But flowers and candlelit dinners were not the Holloway style, and the suggestion to get her something that would lighten her day made him buy her a pair of novelty glasses!

Although Lofty couldn't have loved Michelle and Vicki more, he still wanted a natural child of his own, especially now that his auntie Irene had died. But Michelle aborted his baby, certain that she didn't want to be with Lofty for the rest of her life. To make things worse, she had the operation without even telling him she was pregnant, and her rudeness and insensitivity hurt Lofty deeply.

How could she take away from him the one thing he truly wanted? Suddenly his stutter had gone, and in pain and anger he called her a murderer and said that he hated her. Michelle took his uncharacteristic punishment because she knew she deserved it. He threw her things out on the street, but ironically she would have left him anyway.

He had never felt so wounded and so cheated, and his small amount of pride meant he could not stay. He looked around for work and got a post as a caretaker at a children's home, but before he left the Square he coaxed Sue Osman through labour (albeit through a closed door) and became godfather to little Ali.

Then in April 1988 he gathered together his belongings, and without telling anyone, quietly walked out of Albert Square, a truly tragic figure. He was a thoroughly decent man who never knowingly hurt anyone. His enormous capacity to love was never rewarded, and even though he knew he was a bit of a geek, he knew he never deserved to be treated so badly.

DONNA LUDLOW

Donna was destined for tragedy. Her whole life had been a series of unfortunate and painful mistakes, and it was never going to be long before she gave up the fight.

She was born to a fourteen-year-old Kathy Beale and was the product of a violent rape. Kathy gave her up for adoption, and although she wished her well, she never wanted to see her daughter again.

In 1987, the adoption agency contacted Kathy and told her that her daughter wanted to see her. Kathy turned the offer down, knowing full well that it would only reopen old wounds.

Little did Kathy know, when Donna arrived in town in August of that year, that the rakish waif was in fact her own flesh and blood.

Donna was cunning and, knowing that Kathy didn't want to see her, she used subversive tactics to worm her way into Kathy's affections. She even tried seducing Ian, who was genetically her half-brother, even though she was more interested in Wicksy. She plied Ian for information on his mum, and soon learnt that Kathy was a counsellor for the Samaritans. So Donna started ringing her there, telling her the true-life story of how she wanted to meet her natural mother. Kathy didn't guess who the anonymous caller was until Donna started dropping hints when they bumped into each other round the Square.

Kathy's personal knowledge of one of the callers was in breach of the Samaritans' code of conduct, and she was asked to leave. She became suspicious of Donna, and wondered about her curious interest in Ian. Eventually the two women had a showdown in the flat at Walford Towers, and Kathy demanded to know why Donna was using her son.

'I don't want to get close to him,' Donna said. 'Don't you see? It's you I want to get close to.' And finally the pieces fell into place for Kathy, but the revelation brought her no joy.

Donna couldn't understand why Kathy didn't want to get to know her, and she finally demanded the truth from her mother in June 1988. Kathy didn't want to tell her about the rape – it was her instinct to protect her child from such harmful information – but Donna insisted on learning who her father was. Her childhood fantasy had been that Kathy had been so in love with her father, that Donna's presence only reminded Kath how much of a sham her marriage to Pete was, and that that was why she'd pushed her away.

So when Kathy told her that she had been raped and explained her avoidance of Donna by saying, 'When I

157

look at you all I see is him,' Donna's immediate reaction was disbelief.

But being the conniving schemer that she was, Donna tried to use the truth to her advantage, and told Wicksy in the hope that his pity would lure him away from his girlfriend, Cindy Williams. It didn't, but Donna kept on trying to tempt Wicksy anyway, until her plan backfired and she was sacked from the Vic after a catfight with Cindy in the pub.

Her unemployed status meant she was looking for cheap accommodation, so when Rod Norman suggested they open up a squat in the Square, Donna readily agreed. It meant she could stay near her 'family', and it also meant what little money she had she could spend on her new addiction – heroin.

The Beales came to a tacit acceptance of Donna. She was not part of their family, but they – especially Ian – understood that she wanted some involvement in their lives. They also felt pity for her; behind her lies of success and bliss, it had become obvious to them that Donna was tragically, and perhaps terminally, troubled. Ian gave her a job as a waitress, not just out of pity or duty, but because he had in turn become curious about his half-sister. But when he found out Donna was using heroin, all the old mistrust resurfaced and he sacked her.

Rod too disowned Donna when he couldn't persuade her to kick the habit, and she subsequently became even more bitter than she had ever been before. Her vindictiveness became bitterly twisted with malice and no one was safe from her corruption. She tempted Ali back to the squat with the offer of sex, just so that she could blackmail him later for money to pay for her drugs.

The only person left who would help her was Dot, whose faith gave her the strength to open her door to the lost girl. Dot took Donna in, hoping that her help – and her experience with her son Nick who had also been an addict – would bring Donna back from the brink. But Donna just became evil, spreading spiteful rumours that Colin had left Walford because he had AIDS.

Dot tried to contact Donna's adoptive parents in the hope that they might be able to help her, but they were weak people who were too well versed in their daughter's manipulation to offer anything more than kind – but empty – words.

The heroin made Donna paranoid, and at every aggressive encounter she would fly off the handle and upset herself. She knew she was in a hopeless spiral, and the only person who could stop the downward spin was Kathy.

She agreed to talk to her daughter who begged her to help her. But Kath was adamant and explained that she hadn't asked for Donna and didn't owe her anything. This truth struck home and that evening Donna took a huge hit of heroin and choked on her own vomit.

Dot arrived home to find Donna's lifeless body sprawled on her living-room floor. Both Kathy and Dot felt guilty about Donna's death, feeling there was something that they could have done differently. But in the end they accepted the truth that Donna was tragically scarred by her childhood, and that no one could have been held responsible for her troubles.

DISA O'BRIEN

Diane Butcher befriended Disa when she was living rough on the streets of the West End in 1990. When Diane returned to her family, she didn't expect to ever see Disa again. But as chance would have it, they bumped into each other on the street – when Disa was eight months pregnant!

So when a baby was abandoned on the Butchers' doorstep a few weeks later, Diane quickly put two and two together and sussed out who the little girl belonged to. Against her will, Diane and her boyfriend Mark brought Disa to the Square hoping she would want to get to know her daughter, Billie.

And she did, although it was clear that something was

stopping Disa from showing unconditional love to her daughter, whom she renamed Jasmine. The answer to her resistance became clearer when a mysterious man called Ken asked Dot to pass on £20 to Disa.

It transpired that Ken was Disa's stepfather – the man she had run away from because he had been sexually abusing her. He was also little Jasmine's natural father.

Ken was very good at playing mind games with his stepdaughter, and he tried to gain power over her again by kidnapping her daughter. But Dot the Saviour foiled his wicked intentions, and tricked him into returning to the Square so she could snatch back the child and return her to her mother.

Disa was a confused soul but she found some help when she contacted Kathy at the Samaritans, and with gentle counselling, Disa found the strength to tell her mother, Sandra, about the abuse.

Sandra resolved to take her daughter away from her shabby London life and take her back to Sunderland, where it was hoped that Disa stood a chance of finding happiness.

NIGEL BATES

Nigel was an old school friend of Grant Mitchell, but the two lads never shared much in common. Where Grant was confident, sporty and had luck with the girls, Nigel was insecure, unfit and ridiculed. Nevertheless, now they're grown up, there are a couple of women in Walford who would rather date Nigel than his macho mate.

Nigel is a mummy's boy – and it shows. Not only is he far more sensitive to what women want than any other man in the Square, but he still has no idea how to dress himself!

For years his mother must have bought all his clothes for him, desperate for her little boy not to grow up. And it worked. Not only does he look like an overgrown schoolboy in his ill-fitting suits and novelty ties, but emotionally he still hurts like a child and applies children's values to adult situations.

Consequently, the likes of Grant were quick to ridicule him over the years and so Nigel built a self-defence system of self-mockery, delivering the punchline before anyone else got a chance to tell the joke.

When his mum died in early 1992 he moved in with Dot who was just as keen to have a surrogate son as he was to have a mum. She cooked for him, cleaned for him and in return he respected her – and her home – like no man had ever done before.

Nigel's luck with women turned around in June 1993 when he met Debbie at a party. They sat on the stairs and talked for hours but when Nigel went to the kitchen to get her another drink she disappeared. The Square's natural reaction was one of suspicion – no one could imagine that Nigel could actually pull at a party, and as no one had seen Debbie they were convinced she was a figment of his desperate imagination.

But a couple of weeks later, he saw her filling in on the flower stall for her friend Tracy. His heart leapt. He bought a bunch of flowers from her and gave them straight back – he made no attempt to hide his joy at seeing her again and his enthusiasm swept her off her feet.

They went for several dates – quick drinks or long ambles through the park and they got along famously. As Debbie wasn't from the Square, she hadn't heard the stories of 'nerdy Nigel' and so took him on face value. And on face value he was an extremely nice man. But she still made quick exits saying she had to look after her sick mum. It was Dot who discovered a postcard in Debbie's bag from her fit and healthy mum on holiday, and Nigel realised that yet again he'd been fobbed off.

The fact was that Debbie had been rushing home to care for her eight-year-old daughter, Clare. She hadn't told Nigel about Clare because she was so used to men turning the other way when they found out she had a kid, and as she hadn't expected the relationship to develop, she'd kept her mouth shut.

What she didn't realise is that Nigel is one man who can accept anything as long as it's the truth. Like a child, he believes lying is bad and therefore it wasn't the fact that Debbie had a child that hurt him, it was the fact that she'd lied.

Out of pride he said he never wanted to see her again, even though he was clearly desperate to spend every minute of every day with her. When he finally gave her a chance to explain and apologise, he relented and the next step was to meet Clare. And, naturally, Clare loved him.

The little girl had grown up with an abusive and violent dad, Liam, who would often disappear for months on end and blame her when anything went wrong. And here was this gentle man, who not only bought her ice creams, but made eating them a game rather than a privilege.

Debbie could see that Nigel was perfect for her and her daughter, and the two planned to set up home together.

But one day Debbie didn't show for a date. She didn't call. Nothing. Eventually she turned up in the Square and explained that Liam had returned and she was going to give her marriage yet another try.

Nigel was inconsolable – he had never loved anyone like he'd loved Debbie and it only made things worse knowing that Liam could never make her as happy as he could.

He moped around, deflecting pity by making corny jokes and wearing even wilder ties.

Even though Debbie had decided to leave him alone, Clare couldn't. She didn't understand why mummy wasn't with uncle Nigel any more, and she kept popping up in the Square to see him. Ironically, he was the only one who could explain the situation to her properly. His young-at-heart attitude meant he could communicate with children as very few adults can do. He also told her that she had to go home and that he couldn't see her any more.

Nevertheless, she still came looking for him and one day Debbie followed. A couple of minutes in Nigel's company made her realise that Liam was no comparison, and the next time he raised his fist in violence, she scooped Clare up and made straight for Albert Square.

Although Nigel was over the moon to see her again, he was wary that maybe he was just heading for yet another let-down. So he made Debbie promise that if she stayed the night then she would have to stay forever. 'Can we go to bed now?' was her reply.

The next day she went to collect her things when she knew Liam would be out of their flat, and Nigel prepared his place at number 47 for their permanent occupation. He cleaned, he shopped, he cooked and he waited. And he waited, and finally – late at night – she showed. But she was accompanied by Liam. And he wasn't going to have some 'nerd' steal his woman.

Debbie explained as best she could, but Nigel knew Liam was forcing her to say every untrue word that was coming out of her mouth, and so he lunged at Liam and a scrappy fight ensued. But his bravery could not make up for Liam's brawn and so after the final punch was thrown, Liam left the flat with a tearful Debbie. Nigel was left bloodied and bruised on the floor screaming out after her. But she didn't return.

Despite Nigel's kindness, his sense of humour and his unquestionable morals, he still has relatively few friends in the Square. When he wanted to rent a room at 55 Victoria Road, Michelle did all she could not to laugh at his suggestion. Even Mark, who has no room in life for petty matters, thought twice before renting him Steve's old room at number 47.

The women of Walford think that Nigel is cute, or sweet, and Sharon especially has a soft spot for him, not least because she knows her husband isn't half the friend he ought to be. Most of the men, however, think he's a wimp. The fact that he is one of the few people to have stood up to Nick Cotton (he tried to steal Nigel's stereo when 'collecting' his mum's things from number 25) seems to have been forgotten. But as Grant put it, 'Look at who's sleeping on his own tonight.' Nigel, however, got the last laugh when Debbie returned yet again in January 1994, and this time it looks like she'll stay.

MANDY SALTER

Mandy was born with bad luck running through her veins, but she learnt to compensate by conning and wheedling her way into, and out of, anything.

Her mother was a tart and her dad was nowhere to be seen. She lived virtually by herself on a council estate where she fended for herself using any means necessary. She was smart enough not to get caught by the law (she's smart enough to join Mensa) but she was always in trouble.

She first came to Walford in March 1992 when her mum Lorraine had been so badly beaten she'd ended up in hospital. Lorraine was an acquaintance of Pat's – they'd met in a bar when they'd both been drowning their sorrows – and when Pat saw the state Lorraine was in, she agreed to take care of Mandy for a while. Frank, unsurprisingly, was not best pleased.

For a couple of weeks Mandy was on her best behaviour, offering to do the washing-up and asking before borrowing anything of Sam's. But it soon became clear that Mandy was a little vixen who was constantly on the make. And it didn't take long before Frank had had enough and threw her out. After trying to find her mum – who, it seemed, had run off to Spain with a fella – Mandy returned to the Square and moved in with a grieving Mark at the squat.

She did a good job of ingratiating herself by cooking for him, and even though he only wanted to be left alone with his sadness, Mark realised that Mandy deserved respect. He developed quite a soft spot for her, so when it came to Christmas and she would be spending it on her own, he invited her for turkey and trimmings at the Fowlers'.

Mark, however, was the only East Ender who had

anything nice to say about Mandy. In the few months she'd been in the Square Mandy had rubbed everyone up the wrong way.

She'd come between Sam and Ricky by encouraging Sam to go up West and spend money she couldn't spare. She also tried it on with Ricky and made sure Sam knew about it. Mandy did the same favour for her other so-called best friend, Hattie. First she set Steve up with a girl called Dawn, and when she told Hattie that Steve wanted to see her she timed it perfectly to coincide with Steve and Dawn's first kiss.

Mandy's lack of guidance as a kid means she doesn't know what's off limits, and as the only amusement she can afford is meddling, she doesn't care whether or not she hurts people.

Mark asked his auntie Kathy to take Mandy in for a couple of nights, after Pete's lock-up where she'd been kipping was soaked by the firemen tending to the fire at the Vic. And as it is in Kathy's nature to take on other people's woes, she agreed. Mandy, typically, did nothing about finding somewhere permanent to stay, realising she was on a cushy number with Kath. But she did worse than simply outstay her welcome; she abused her hostess's goodwill by turning her flat into a pigsty, and bad mouthing her to all the Square. She told them how Kathy treated her like a slave, ordering her to do the nastiest chores. Of course it was untrue, but Mandy was very cunning at seizing every opportunity to manipulate people to her advantage. Only this time it backfired because when Kathy found out what she'd been saying, she was out on her ear.

Pete was another of the Beale/Fowler clan to help her out, but she thanked him for giving her a job on his stall by stealing his takings. Pete forgave her, and even offered her more work, when he saw that she'd been sleeping rough in the Square gardens.

As if it wasn't enough for the whole of Walford to feel sorry for her, Mandy felt sorry for herself too. She never forgave her mum for not turning up – or even sending a present – at Christmas 1992, and she felt as if she was owed something. And as she'd never been close to anyone, she just couldn't give a damn about hurting anyone.

She moved in with Mark again when he rented a flat at number 47 and she stayed there until she shacked up with would-be footballer Aidan Brosnan, and Mark had to tell her that the flat just wasn't big enough for all of them.

So Mandy and Aidan opened up the derelict building at number 5, and made their squat their palace. Even though they weren't paying rent, money was still in very short supply and Mandy had to use all her cunning to keep their heads above water.

It was no wonder she didn't tell Aidan how she was making cash, because she knew he'd be hurt (although he'd be too much of a wimp to do anything about it). She'd been going up to King's Cross – a notorious red light district – and clipping (taking the money from 'clients' and running before they demanded services). But when she got beaten up by some prostitutes who thought she was giving them a bad name, Mandy gave it up.

Mrs Andreas gave them both jobs shelf-filling in First Til Last and it was here that Mandy overheard Grant telling Nigel about Den being Vicki's father. This was the best bit of gossip she'd ever heard and it was with glee that she spread it round the Square.

When Mrs Andreas's nephew came to London he was given their jobs and so once again Mandy and Aidan were penniless. The young lovers made ends meet by doing odd jobs round the Square for breakfast or a fiver. When Grant couldn't be bothered to take Roly for a walk, he lobbed her a handout and she disappeared with the dog. But in October 1993 it ended up costing Grant far more than a fiver when Mandy let Roly off the lead and he ran in front of a van and was killed.

Mandy had never known anything but a tough life, but Aidan was accustomed to a few luxuries – like a roof over his head – and his grubby life in Albert Square got him down. So when they were evicted from the squat just before Christmas, it was the final straw for him.

With his career in football over, he saw no hope in the future, and he'd lost all pride living with Mandy. He decided to end it all and planned to kill himself by jumping off the roof of a high-rise building. But Mandy persuaded him that he was better than he thought, and she told him that she loved him, and he relented. Finally, she had done one entirely good deed, if not entirely selflessly.

Aidan packed his bags afterwards and returned to his native Ireland, Mandy meanwhile was taken in by the Fowlers. The residents of Albert Square – no matter how much she'd conned them and infuriated them – felt guilty that she'd been homeless at Christmas, and here and there people gave her fivers and tenners to see her right.

She had been so moved by what happened with Aidan – he had made her realise that she could really feel something for someone – that she saved the money she was given so she could join him in Ireland. And in January 1994 she too waved bye-bye to Walford. But not many tears were shed because everyone's worried that one day she'll come back!

WEDDINGS

They say it's the most important day of your life, but if you're a resident of Albert Square, you can bet your wedding day will also be your most traumatic!

Elopements, jiltings, marriages of convenience, family bust-ups and good old bun fights – an East End wedding is never as easy as saying 'I do'.

MICHELLE FOWLER AND LOFTY HOLLOWAY, 25 SEPTEMBER 1986

Everybody knew it was a marriage of convenience – she wanted a father for her baby and he wanted someone to love. Even so, everybody in Albert Square wished Lofty and Michelle all the luck in the world, because if anyone in Walford could have used a bit of happiness it was these two.

Lofty's stag night was entirely forgettable – if you'd had as much to drink as Lofty had! His hangover on his wedding morning was the worst of his life, but little did he know his headache was about to get worse. Chivvied by Wicksy (who was wearing a T-shirt with the legend 'I survived Lofty's stag night – just!'), Lofty struggled into his hired morning suit.

Michelle on the other hand was feeling a little perkier. The shenanigans of her hen night may have been led by Angie, but just about the wildest thing they got up to was an X-rated version of pin the tail on the donkey!

She wandered around in her curlers and dressing gown until the last minute, before putting on the white wedding dress that Kathy had made for her. Lofty meanwhile was getting undressed because he said he felt like a penguin in the hired suit. Instead he made his way to the church in his familiar tweed jacket.

Michelle handed Vicki over to Kathy to mind during the service, and the Fowlers and the rest of the Square made their way to St Luke's church to wait for Michelle's arrival.

Den and Angie sat in the pews with the rest of the congregation, but it was clear Den was restless. Maybe he felt guilty because he knew that if it hadn't been for him, Michelle would not have been getting married at seventeen.

Whatever his reasons, he made a quick excuse to Ange and said he had to pop out, but promised he'd be back in time for the service.

As Lofty made his way to the church, Den was scuttling back to the Square, and just before Michelle was due to leave there was a knock at her bedroom door.

She expected it to be Arthur, proud as punch to be giving his only daughter away, but when Michelle turned round it was Den who was standing in the doorway.

He'd come to tell her that he loved her. Michelle was too worried that either Arthur or Sharon (her bridesmaid) would catch them together to take in what he was saying. But when he gave her a gold pendant ('something new'), she understood perfectly what he meant. He made a quick exit, but was too cut up to go back to St Luke's.

The wedding car that Arthur couldn't afford (he'd stolen £1,514 from the Square's Christmas Club fund to pay for the nuptials) arrived to take the bridal party to the church. Michelle got her flowers out of the fridge and got into the car, but she was very quiet during the short journey. She was tormented by what Den had said, but it was too late now, she knew she would have to go through with the wedding and keep Den's love for her memories.

Lofty waited nervously at the altar and Wicksy did the best man's job of calming the groom down. Just as Lofty was beginning to think that Michelle wasn't coming, he turned to the back of the church to see his beautiful bride and he filled with pride and relief.

The music started, Arthur took Michelle's arm and Sharon arranged herself for the walk down the aisle. But the bride stood motionless, clutching her new pendant in her hand. Michelle looked at her dad and told him simply that she couldn't do it, and gently, Arthur led his daughter away from the scene of her crime.

Lofty took it well, considering. The Square rallied round him, and he managed to hold it together until he was left alone that evening when he finally broke down in tears. A few days later he suffered a severe asthma attack which Dr Legg put down to stress. Michelle, naturally, felt guilty.

Michelle could offer no explanation for jilting Lofty, but the East Enders displayed a strange lack of curiosity – it was as if they had been expecting it. It was only when Den went to Venice to make a go of things with Angie, that Michelle was forced to realise she would never have Den for herself. And so on 25 November she finally married Lofty in a registry office. But it wouldn't be long before she wished she'd jilted him a second time.

CARMEL ROBERTS AND MATTHEW JACKSON, 24 JANUARY 1989

Health visitor Carmel had always been a beast of burden, coping with other people's problems when they had run out of faith and strength. But when she married Matthew Jackson, she was getting massive problems of her own to cope with.

He seemed like the perfect guy. He was good-looking, did the washing-up, bought flowers and tolerated her niece and nephew who were constantly dumped on them. But Mr Wonderful started to show his true colours on the day of the wedding. Unfortunately it was too late for Carmel to have second thoughts.

She thought she'd surprise Matthew by inviting his

mum, Lynne, to the registry office service. He was surprised all right, but he was also very angry. He made his vows through pursed lips, and as soon as the wedding was over he grabbed his new wife and shook her violently, chastising her like a difficult toddler.

Carmel was so distressed by her husband's actions (and so ashamed) that she could not face the reception. Matthew could not face his mother. So the newlyweds made straight for their honeymoon.

When they returned to the Square, it soon became clear that Matthew had very violent tendencies, and after one very severe beating a few months later, Carmel knew her marriage was over.

PAT WICKS AND FRANK BUTCHER, 22 JUNE 1989

Pat and Frank's knot-tying was one of the happiest occasions the East Enders have celebrated – it's also the only wedding that's led to a truly happy marriage.

Even though Pat and Frank had both been married before (twice in Pat's case), they still wanted to make their wedding extra-special. Frank's mum Mo was put in charge of the organising – and she did her son proud. Trestles were set up in the Square and the reception turned into a street party to which all the neighbours were invited.

But not everyone was playing happy families. Pat's ex-husband, Pete Beale, escorted his estranged wife Kathy; and Pat's son Simon came on the arm of Sharon, the woman whose heart he was about to break. But for a few hours at least the feuds stopped, worries were forgotten and troubles were drowned with a singsong in the pub around Wicksy's piano.

Although Pat was a June bride, the weather was far from seasonal. The sun may have been shining, but a vicious wind whipped round the houses and lifted a few hemlines, baring flesh to a bitter chill. But as Pat and

Frank had their love to keep them warm, the weather didn't really matter!

CINDY WILLIAMS AND IAN BEALE, 12 OCTOBER 1989

When Cindy told Ian she was pregnant, he was over the moon. But the smile would have quickly disappeared from his face if he'd known that he wasn't the baby's father.

Then again, after the debacle of the wedding, he might just have seen the funny side of it . . .

None of Ian's family liked Cindy, and although they tried their hardest, they just couldn't put their feelings on hold for the day. Cindy's flagrant red dress – which did nothing to downplay her fertile bump – was like a rag to a bull. And the bull on this occasion was, unsurprisingly, Pete Beale. The two of them squabbled childishly as Ian looked on, helpless to stop the point-scoring. It was hard to believe he was old enough to be getting married – he barely looked old enough to be the pageboy, let alone the groom of an expectant mother.

Ironically, Ian's choice for best man was the secret father of Cindy's baby, Simon Wicks. Naturally enough, Wicksy found the role of best man uncomfortable. But it was Cindy who was feeling the most awkward: she was marrying a man she knew she didn't love in the hope that Wicksy would get jealous enough to claim her for himself. But his loyalty to the Beales meant that wasn't going to happen, and when Cindy realised this she began to feel like a fool. But instead of showing remorse, she put on a show of single-mindedness which led her to slap Pete round the face and slag off the rest of her in-laws.

After the service they returned to the flat in Walford Towers for a reception of sorts, where her behaviour went from bad to worse. In the end even Ian had had enough. He was so disgusted with her behaviour that he stormed out, leaving her sobbing in the flat to spend her wedding night alone.

Sadly, the marriage was little better than the wedding, and it wasn't long before Cindy was forced to tell Ian the truth about Wicksy and Steven. Ian was distraught at her revelation and drove off into the night as if he was trying to get away from the truth. In a fit of rage he crashed his car and ended up in intensive care with several broken bones. When he regained consciousness he seemed to remember nothing, but Cindy, unable to face her husband and his family, ran off to her parents' house in Devon. Wicksy, shame-faced, followed her.

When Ian was discharged from hospital, his dad persuaded him to go to Devon to try and save his marriage. But when he saw that Wicksy was there he went on a drinking binge. In his drunkenness he hurled a brick – and one of his crutches – through a window at the illicit lovers, who calmly reacted by inviting him in. But thanks to the amount of alcohol Ian had consumed, he passed out before they had to indulge in difficult conversation.

The next day, Ian stole Cindy's dad's shotgun and returned to the Square to rid memories of Steven and Cindy from his life. But they followed him back to Walford to face the music. A blood test confirmed what everyone knew was true, and it seemed that Ian had accepted the truth. But in fact he was plotting his own warped and twisted revenge.

Ian thought he had found the answer when he tampered with the brakes on his delivery van in the hope that he could kill both himself and Wicksy.

They both survived the crash, but when Cindy and Wicksy realised the extremes Ian was capable of, they packed up and left the Square in December 1990. Ian, on the other hand, couldn't escape the memories and in 1992, he tracked his wife down and brought her back to the Square.

Mercifully, there weren't quite as many fireworks the second time around!

When these two teenagers announced their engagement in May 1991, the hostility from their families was so intense that they were banned from seeing each other. So they hatched a plot that would free them from the clutches of their families – and decided to elope.

Sam disguised herself in a black bobbed wig so that her mum wouldn't recognise her as she left the school gates, and unseen she walked round the corner and into Ricky's van. Together at last, they headed north for a secret wedding ceremony in Gretna Green.

As soon as the Mitchells and the Butchers realised the kids were missing, they sussed that they were together. And when Grant and Phil found the RAC route map to Gretna Green left lying in the repair shop, they had a pretty good idea of Sam and Ricky's destination – and their intention.

They grabbed their car keys and tipped off the Butchers before following the young lovers in hot pursuit. Frank and Pat got to their action stations and jumped in their car to join the chase. But just in case, Pat picked out a nice frock anyway.

When Sam and Ricky got to Gretna Green they were in for a let-down: things didn't happen in reality as easily as they did in folklore and getting hitched was going to take a lot longer than they'd expected. An official at the registry office told them soberly that there was a two-week waiting period.

Of course they hadn't enough money to survive for two weeks, but they were determined to seal their union and defy their folks. And so they slept in the back of Ricky's van – which had been painted to avoid detection – until their turn to say 'I do' came round.

Meanwhile, the Mitchells and the Butchers had been forced to accept defeat, but Grant made the most of the situation by booking a date for him and Sharon.

By chance, Sam bumped into Pat in the ladies' of a

petrol station and was surprised to learn that Pat was sympathetic to their cause. So Sam let her in on the secret and Pat responded by giving her 'a little something' to make sure they had enough to eat before the big day.

And on 4 July, the waiting was over and Sam and Ricky exchanged vows with Sam wearing a dress she'd borrowed from a fellow runaway.

On their return to Albert Square, Frank and Sam's mum Peggy were forced to accept the marriage and decided to make it 'proper' by arranging a church blessing for the newlyweds. And on 25 July, they did it all again at St Stephen's parish church in Walford. Unfortunately – and typically – the blessing clashed with the funeral service for Charlie Cotton.

SHARON WATTS AND GRANT MITCHELL, 26 DECEMBER 1991

Grant had always had it in mind to marry Sharon just as soon as he could. For her, though, the marriage came just a little too soon.

Grant surprised Sharon with a proposal on his return from Gretna Green after trying to stop his little sister Sam marrying his apprentice, Ricky. But the teen lovers had obviously put him in the marrying mood, and while he was in Scotland he'd bought a marriage licence.

Sharon agreed to the wedding but the plans had to be put on ice when she got the temporary tenancy of the Vic following Eddie Royle's murder. Grant, however, decided that he couldn't wait any longer than he had to, and set about organising a surprise wedding for his fiancée.

On Boxing Day morning he woke Sharon early and told her he had something special planned. He'd bought a dress and flowers and all he needed now was Sharon's consent.

But she wasn't sure. She didn't want to be rushed into marriage and so she turned to her good pal Michelle

Fowler for advice. It would have been reasonable to expect Michelle to have encouraged Sharon to turn her lover down (Michelle and Grant bicker with each other like playground rivals), but instead Michelle just asked her friend a simple question: 'Do you love him?'

Sharon decided that she did, and that all they were doing was tying the knot earlier rather than later, and the romance of Grant's impetuousness made up for all their warring.

And so she went to the registry office – with Michelle returning the favour and being her bridesmaid – and married Grant with a smile on her face: she knew she was signing up for a lifetime of surprises. Unfortunately not all of them would be as welcome as her Boxing Day wedding.

GILL ROBINSON AND MARK FOWLER, 23 JUNE 1992

Even though Mark knew that Gill didn't have long to live before she died of an AIDS-related cancer, he still wanted to marry her before the end came. In secret, he arranged for a special marriage licence, and on the morning of 23 June 1993 he asked her to be his wife.

She thought he was crazy. Then she thought it was just his idea of a joke. And then, with a little gentle persuading from her nurse George, she agreed.

Delighted, Mark returned to the Square from the hospice where Gill was being cared for to tell his sister Michelle that he was marrying Gill at three o'clock that afternoon. 'But why?' was her reply. Mark gave her the only reason that mattered – because they loved each other. And anyway, he wanted to make her last few days as happy as possible.

While George rigged Gill up with a cocktail of drugs that would keep the pain away for the duration of the service, Mark and Michelle sorted through Gill's things so Mark could take an overnight bag for the 'honeymoon'.

'Have you got a ring?' Michelle asked. Mark had completely forgotten, but it was all right, because Michelle had her wedding ring in her hand and was offering it as a wedding present. 'I'd like to see it going to a good marriage,' she said.

And it was a good marriage. Mark and Gill did everything to please each other, put the other before themselves. And they made each other laugh.

At the registry office, Gill got out of her wheelchair to say her vows and Mark supported her with a firm arm around her waist. The only wedding guests were George, Michelle, and Mark's former girlfriend Rachel. And as they looked on with affection and pride the registrar pronounced them man and wife.

Their wedding supper was at a local hotel. When the waiter brought the menu round, Gill decided the only thing she felt well enough to eat was ice cream. And as it was her day, Mark, Michelle and Rachel also ordered sundaes and the four of them chatted and laughed until Michelle and Rachel made a polite exit to let Mark and Gill enjoy their wedding night.

Because Gill was so weak, Mark had no choice but to carry her over the threshold – but he would have done it anyway. He laid her down on the bed and soon realised that the day had been too much for her. She had become weak and was fading fast.

He called for an ambulance which came quickly to take Gill back to the hospice where, the next day, Mark watched his bride die.

NADIA AND PHIL MITCHELL,
8 JULY 1993

Normally, a groom is supposed to be in love with his wife on his wedding day, but Phil Mitchell was in love with his brother's wife.

Sharon's decision to go back to Grant was a rejection Phil absorbed like a boxer taking a body blow – he made it to the end of the fight, but it sure did hurt the next day. And the next.

In fact Phil was so down that he became a bit of a masochist. He wanted to believe in love so badly that he gave spurned Hattie Tavernier a no-srings ride to Southampton to see if she could patch things up with her boyfriend, Steve Elliot. And when he met Nadia – an illegal Romanian immigrant – in a wine bar and heard how she would be deported and separated from her boyfriend, Marcus, he decided to marry her so that their love could stand a chance.

He took Nadia back to Walford with him, and she stayed with him at the Vic until a registry-office wedding could be arranged. Sharon, unjustifiably, felt that her nose had been put out of joint and she became curious about the arrangement as she just didn't believe they were in love.

And so Phil was forced to let Sharon in on the secret, as well as Nigel and Grant who both came to the wedding.

Phil wore his best suit with a yellow carnation in his buttonhole, and Nadia looked lovely in an off-white dress. After the quick service, a couple of photos were taken – so as to fool the Home Office if need be – and Nadia disappeared.

Phil didn't expect to hear from his wife again until it was time to get a divorce, in fact he practically forgot that he was married at all. He just saw it as doing someone a favour, saving Nadia the heartbreak of being separated from Marcos – who also had an arranged marriage – and the misery of being deported to a country she hated.

He therefore didn't consider telling Kathy when they started to date. So when Nadia reared her head in the Square again in November, Phil had some tricky explaining to do.

Although he managed to fool the Home Office for a while, Kathy was deeply suspicious and hurt. Immigration officials also kept a suspicious eye on the 'newlyweds' who had been forced to live together to avoid prosecution. During this time, Nadia realised that Phil was her dream ticket to happiness and schemed to make their relationship slightly less 'arranged'. She flirted with him and tried to make him fall in love with her. And on Christmas Day, they finally consummated their marriage when Phil was very drunk, and Nadia was very keen.

But even sex could not make this a real marriage. However, as long as the immigration officials never twig, Phil and Nadia both have a happy future ahead of them – apart.

CALENDAR OF EVENTS

1985

FEBRUARY

Reg Cox is found in his bedsit on the 19th and later dies. Pauline Fowler discovers she's pregnant again at 42 – and Lou isn't pleased.

MARCH

Mary and Annie move into Reg's room on the 5th. Racist graffiti is daubed on the convenience store and Nick Cotton is the prime suspect.

APRIL

Mark disappears on the 18th. Naima confesses she doesn't sleep with her husband Saeed. Debs starts the Save Our Square campaign to stop redevelopment. Angie discovers Den is in Spain with Jan.

MAY

Sharon wants to go on the Pill and sleep with Kelvin. Chris Smith arrives to visit his daughter Mary.

JUNE

Lou moves in with Pete as Pauline is too stressed. On the 20th, Sue and Ali find their son Hassan has died in his cot.

JULY

Dot appears in the launderette for the first time on the 4th. Michelle accidentally dyes Lofty's hair green!

AUGUST

Martin Fowler is born on the 1st. Sue gives the Fowlers Hassan's clothes. Mary is caught shoplifting. Michelle is feeling unloved and looks for comfort with several men round the Square. She finds it with Den on the 22nd when they secretly make love.

SEPTEMBER

Debs and Andy are burgled just after their insurance policy runs out. Martin's christening is postponed because the lad has gastro-enteritis. Michelle confides to Lou that she's pregnant.

OCTOBER

On the 3rd, Michelle meets Den – the secret father of her baby – by the canal. Wicksy arrives in his spitfire on the 8th. Nick Cotton steals Kathy's medical notes.

NOVEMBER

Nick is blackmailing Kathy about the kid she had when she was fourteen. Ian wins a boxing match. Kath breaks down at the Vic and confesses to Angie and Pauline that she was raped and had a child as a teenager. Pete gets angry when he is told the news on the 12th.

Lou is frustrated at having to use a commode. Angie crashes Den's car while drunk. Mary strips unaware that Saeed is in the audience. Cassie Carpenter arrives on Boxing Day covered in bruises – she says her mum's boyfriend Neville has been hitting her. Michelle, Pauline and Arthur go to Southend to look for Mark.

1986

JANUARY

The Fowlers find Mark working in an amusement park. He is living with an older woman whose kids call him 'daddy'. On the 30th, Jan enters the Vic during a drag night.

FEBRUARY

Den moves in with Jan. Lofty proposes to Michelle. Wicksy confesses he's in trouble with a loan shark, and Pete lends him £1,500. Angie is depressed about Den and gathers together pills from her friends. On the 27th she takes an overdose.

MARCH

Angie's friends take turns keeping an eye on her. Dot is thrilled when Charlie turns up, but he steals from her and leaves again. Sgt Quick proposes to Debs while Andy teaches Mary to read.

APRIL

On the 8th Michelle agrees to marry Lofty as Ian and Sharon start dating. Den and Angie go on holiday to Ibiza, but he returns without her. Arthur starts a

Christmas Club fund for his neighbours. On her return, Angie sleeps with Andy.

MAY

Ali and Mehmet start up Ozcabs. Dot wins £250 at bingo and Nick steals her chequebook. Sharon runs away (she is actually staying at Mary's). Michelle gives birth to Vicki on the 27th and Den visits them in hospital.

JUNE

Michelle, Sharon and Ian all take their O-levels. Kelvin plans to form a band with his socialist friends from college, Harry and Tessa. Pat Wicks arrives on the 12th and tells Pete that Simon's not his son. Arthur is worrying about paying for Michelle's wedding.

JULY

Mark returns to the Square with his friend Owen. They share a joint with Cassie Carpenter and a feud starts between the Fowlers and the Carpenters.

AUGUST

A reunited Debs and Andy argue. She tells him to 'drop dead' as he storms out to work on the 14th, and is later killed saving a child from being run over. Colin moves into number 3 on the 3rd. Dog Market play their first gig at the Vic and Den bans them. They rename themselves The Banned.

SEPTEMBER

The Fowlers are broken into and the Christmas Club money is stolen. Pauline twigs that Arthur has faked the break-in because he has taken the money. On the 25th Michelle jilts Lofty at the altar.

OCTOBER

Angie is depressed as she believes she has lost Den for good. When he asks for a divorce on the 16th, she tells him she only has six months to live. Kathy starts a knitting stall in the market.

NOVEMBER

The Walford Attacker is at large. On the 13th, Arthur is arrested and confesses to the break-in. Den takes Angie to Venice on the 18th where they accidentally bump into Jan. Lofty and Michelle say 'I do' on the 25th, the same day that Den overhears Angie confessing her lie about dying.

DECEMBER

Kelvin starts an affair with an older woman, Carmel Roberts. James Willmott-Brown buys Debbie's house. Den gives Angie divorce papers as a Christmas present. Pauline sees Michelle with Den on Christmas Day and twigs he is Vicki's father. Arthur breaks down that evening and smashes up the Fowler house.

1987

JANUARY

Arthur is admitted into hospital. Mary is beaten up by fellow prostitutes. Mehmet rips off Kathy and Michelle for £2,000 on a bogus deal with Kath's jumpers. Dr Singh prescribes hormone treatment for menopausal Dot.

FEBRUARY

Willmott-Brown buys the Dagmar. On the 17th, a lynch mob metes out natural justice on Mehmet. On the 19th, Pat is viciously beaten by the Walford Attacker. Jan is behind the bar at the Vic, but she is not enjoying her new job and on the 26th she walks out.

MARCH

Pete again has no alibi when another woman is attacked and he is questioned by the police. Angie gets the job as manageress at the Dagmar. Arthur comes home from the hospital and tells Pauline he's the luckiest man in the world to have her as his wife. Kathy starts at the Samaritans.

APRIL

The adoption agency tells Kathy her daughter wants to see her, but Kathy's not interested. The Attacker is caught when he pounces on Debs in the launderette. She becomes engaged to the investigating officer, Sgt Terry Rich. Sharon and Wicksy go away for a dirty weekend, but Simon ends up on the sofa when Sharon decides to hold on to her virginity. Mary leaves Annie on her own and the toddler accidentally starts a fire.

MAY

Arthur's trial begins and he is sentenced to 28 days. Den starts an affair with Magda Czajkowski. On the 14th, Chris and Edie Smith take Annie to Stockport with them. Pauline eavesdrops on Den and Michelle arguing in the launderette, and her suspicions are confirmed. Tony leaves for the Caribbean on the 28th.

JUNE

Barry tells his brother Graham that he's gay, but Graham has already guessed. The Dagmar reopens on the 25th and evening trade slackens at the Vic. Den gets a video jukebox in that attracts drug pushers. Michelle doesn't know how to comfort Lofty when his auntie Irene dies on the 18th.

JULY

Naima meets another cousin that her family have sent her as a prospective husband, but to her surprise she likes Farrukh. The Firm send Den to Morocco on a courier job. In his absence Wicksy flirts with Mags. Carmel moves into number 3.

AUGUST

Mags moves into Kelvin's old flat. Michelle tells a depressed Den that she'll go away with him because she is bored with Lofty. Donna arrives and flirts with every man she meets. The Vic beats the Dagmar at five-a-side football by cheating. Rod moves in with Mary.

SEPTEMBER

The ladies' darts team have a day trip to Greenwich where Pat meets up with old flame Frank Butcher who asks her to marry him. Donna gets a job at the Vic.

OCTOBER

Sharon sets Den and Angie up on a date and they end up in bed together. The next day they – unconvincingly – say it was for old times' sake. Sharon is feeling neglected and goes to church where she meets Duncan the curate on her 18th birthday. Nick and Charlie turn up on Dot's doorstep and meet for the first time. Sue tells Ali that at last she is pregnant again.

NOVEMBER

Angie returns to the Queen Vic in a 'business only' partnership with Den. Everyone gets food poisoning from Ian's food on Bonfire Night – he has used knock-off salmon from Charlie. Chris finally brings Annie back to an overjoyed Mary.

DECEMBER

Colin sends Barry to tell his dad that he's gay. Sharon gets engaged to Duncan. A drunken Chris Smith kidnaps baby Annie, but crashes his lorry before he makes it out of the Square. Annie, thankfully, isn't hurt. Michelle confides in Pauline that she is pregnant.

1988

JANUARY

Michelle has an abortion which Den pays for. When Pauline tells Lofty he is broken-hearted. He later throws Michelle out of their flat. Den admits to Pauline he is Vicki's father. The Karims take over at First Til Last.

FEBRUARY

Kenny Beale arrives from New Zealand and faces the music about Wicksy's paternity. Barry and Ian go into business together running mobile discos. Donna calls Kathy at the Samaritans.

MARCH

Den visits Angie who has been in hospital for kidney failure and they talk about setting up together in a new pub away from Walford. Kathy starts work at the Dagmar. Sue gives birth to little Ali on the 24th.

APRIL

Kathy faces her past on the 14th when Donna reveals she is her daughter. Lofty leaves to start a job as a caretaker in a children's home. On the 21st, Tom collapses and dies in the Vic.

MAY

Willmott-Brown is obviously taken with Kathy and makes Pete jealous by buying her presents. Den buys one of the flats at number 43 for Sharon, Michelle and Vicki. Mary leaves the Square for good, as does Angie who runs off to Spain with Sonny.

JUNE

The Firm open Strokes wine bar and Den is installed as chief pint-puller. Pat and Frank take over at the Vic. Donna's persistence forces Kath to tell her that she is a product of a rape. Wicksy starts seeing Cindy Williams.

JULY

While Pete is on holiday with his mum on the 7th, Willmott-Brown invites Kathy for an after-hours drink and rapes her. The Dagmar is burnt to the ground and Den is seen looking on. Lou gathers her clan together and gives out her heirlooms and advice. On the 21st she dies in her sleep.

AUGUST

Ian gets his catering qualifications and starts working for Ali. Donna and Cindy have a cat fight and Frank sacks Donna. The Firm ask Den to take the heat for the fire at the Dagmar and so he goes on the run.

SEPTEMBER

Matthew moves in with Carmel while Mo moves into the Vic where she clashes with Pat. Den gives himself up and he is held in Dickens Hill prison on remand.

OCTOBER

Dot starts a Neighbourhood Watch scheme. Michelle becomes close to Dr David Samuels. Ricky flirts with Shireen while she babysits for the Fowlers.

NOVEMBER

Sharon visits her dad in prison and she is shocked to see he has been beaten up for grassing. Donna starts using heroin and Rod's protests won't stop her. Kathy and Pete return from a holiday that was meant to be a tonic after the rape, but Kathy says she won't sleep with her husband again.

DECEMBER

In jail, Nick confesses to Den that he killed Reg Cox. Rod tells Ian about Donna's drug dependency and Ian fires her. Guido Smith moves in with Colin. Donna tricks Ali into having sex with her so she can blackmail him.

1989

JANUARY

The police catch Willmott-Brown trying to bribe Kath.
Dr Legg tells Colin he has multiple sclerosis. The regulars
have a sit-in in the Queen Vic to demand all-day opening.
On the 24th, Carmel and Matthew get married.

FEBRUARY

Ian and Cindy announce their engagement. Colin leaves
Walford for Bristol. Den is kidnapped by the Firm on the
way to his trial, but he escapes their clutches and arranges
to meet Michelle at the canal on the 23rd. The Firm have
Michelle followed by gunmen, and after their meeting
Den is shot and it seems he has died.

MARCH

Hazel knocks on Dot's door holding a baby that she says
is Nick's. Carmel and Matthew have to look after Junior
and Ayisha full-time, and Matthew's temper comes to the
surface. Frank opens the car lot and sells Ian a jeep. The
police tell Michelle and Sharon – who are both wearing
fancy-dress costumes – that Den is almost certainly dead.

APRIL

After Kathy makes it clear she doesn't want to see her
daughter, Donna takes an overdose and dies in Dot's

living room on the 13th. Kathy's trauma continues at Willmott-Brown's trial where she gives evidence. He is convicted and sentenced to three years. Michelle tells Sharon that Den is Vicki's father. Sharon is very hurt and runs away.

MAY

Cindy and Wicksy make love after closing in the Vic. Pat finally divorces Brian Wicks. Vicki has meningitis and is rushed to hospital. Michelle keeps a 24-hour vigil and is there when Sharon visits. They say little to each other but hug before Sharon disappears again. Matthew violently beats Carmel. Sue breaks down; Ali finds her at Hassan's grave and she is taken in a mental hospital.

JUNE

Arthur takes part in a TV quiz called *Cat and Mouse* and wins a holiday. Julie Cooper moves into the Karims' house. Charlie discovers that Hazel has been lying to Dot in order to get some money out of her. The baby isn't Nick's at all – it's Hazel's sister's. Ian takes control of the café. On the 22nd Pat and Frank marry in style. Dot meets Charlie's other wife, Joan.

JULY

Frank's troublesome daughter Janine comes to live at the Vic. Paul Priestley converts the chip shop in Turpin Road into Julie's hairdressing salon. An enraged Matthew fights with Carmel. Junior saves his aunt by stabbing and badly hurting Matthew. Pete wins £1,000 on premium bonds.

AUGUST

Pete uses his windfall to go to New Zealand to visit Kenny. Michelle starts seeing another older man, Danny Whiting, who is married with three kids. Cindy is trying to get Wicksy to go out with her. Julie offers Michelle a job at the salon. Janine runs away.

SEPTEMBER

Frank finds Janine camping out in one of the cars on the lot. New fruit and veg stall-holder Laurie Bates makes a play for Kath. Pauline and Arthur take their prize holiday to Minorca. Wicksy moves in with Sharon.

OCTOBER

Cindy and Ian have the wedding from hell on the 12th. It seems he might file for divorce before the day is over! Ali is thrown out of his flat – and thus the Square – by landlord Alan McIntyre. The Butchers buy the B&B from Doris.

NOVEMBER

Stella, Ashraf Karim's mistress, meets her lover secretly in Walford. Marge is mugged; Michelle's boyfriend Danny is the only witness, however, and he refuses to give his name to the police. Dot starts a clean-up campaign when she spies a rat.

DECEMBER

Pauline goes into hospital to have a hysterectomy. Michelle's Christmas is tainted when she opens a card from

Danny which was meant for his wife. On the 26th, Cindy gives birth prematurely to Steven and Wicksy is torn when he sees the child.

1990

JANUARY

When Diane believes everyone has forgotten her birthday (they were planning a surprise party) she runs away. Frank is distraught. Danny convinces Michelle to move to Newcastle with him. Barbara arrives from New Zealand to see Pete.

FEBRUARY

At the last minute, Michelle backs out of leaving for Newcastle. The Mitchell brothers set up shop underneath the Arches. Rod and Hazel leave to go travelling in India.

MARCH

Nick returns and appears to be a reformed character. He even claims to be a born-again Christian – but he's really trying to get his hands on Dot's £10,000 bingo winnings. Diane comes back to the Square with a middle-aged photographer – Taylor – in tow.

APRIL

Nick insists on cooking all of Dot's meals for her. He says they will cure her ailments but in fact he is slowly poisoning her. Shireen Karim meets Jabbar, the boy her family has arranged for her to marry. A body that could be Den's is pulled out of the canal. Sharon is too upset and leaves Michelle to take care of the burial arrangements.

MAY

Sharon decides to search for her natural parents. Money worries mean the Butchers have to give up the tenancy at the Vic, and Sharon thinks the lease will come to her. Charlie discovers Nick's poison, but Dot refuses to press charges.

JUNE

Ashraf continues to see Stella and the Karims leave Walford for Bristol. The council plan to close down the market. While Pete protests, Michelle and Kathy prove the council boss, Kendle, is crooked. Kathy twigs about Cindy and Wicksy.

JULY

Eddie Royle takes over the reins at the Vic. The Taverniers move into number 27. Diane paints a mural on the side of number 18 while her family is on holiday. Sharon finally meets her mother, Carol Hanley, who has just given birth to another baby. Her husband Ron persuades Sharon to keep her distance.

AUGUST

Cindy tells Ian the truth about Wicksy and Steven. Ian is destroyed by the revelation and drives off in a fury. He crashes and ends up in intensive care.

SEPTEMBER

When Ian is discharged he follows Cindy to her parents' house in Devon. Wicksy is there but a fight is avoided when Ian passes out drunk. The next morning he takes Cindy's dad's shotgun and returns to the Square. Cindy and Simon also come back to Walford to lay the matter to rest. Mark comes home out of the blue. His family is ecstatic but it is clear he is hiding a secret.

OCTOBER

A blood test proves Simon is Steven's father. An increasingly senile Mo starts a fire in her house but tragedy is avoided when Mark rescues her.

NOVEMBER

Mark and Diane become close, as do Sharon and Grant as they haggle over the selling price of her flat. Ian's business is taking off and he hires his mum to take over the café. Money is missing from the tills at the Vic.

DECEMBER

Clyde Tavernier takes custody of his son Kofi and brings the boy to live in Albert Square. Ian offers Wicksy extra work, but he actually plans to kill Simon (and himself) by crashing the van on a delivery. It transpires that Ian had taken the money from the Vic in order to frame Wicksy. Cindy and Simon realised they must leave Walford. A baby is abandoned on Diane's doorstep.

1991

JANUARY

The baby, Billie, belongs to Diane's homeless friend Disa. Ian is becoming hard-hearted and thick skinned and is isolating himself from everyone in the Square. Eddie's old girlfriend Eibhlín arrives and puts Kathy's nose out of joint. Mark tells Diane he is HIV positive. Billie is kidnapped by Disa's step-dad Ken.

FEBRUARY

Dot rescues Billie and Disa leaves for a new life in Sunderland with her daughter. Mark and Arthur get the contract to tend the Square gardens. Everyone but Mark forgets Ethel's seventy-fifth birthday. Etta's career ambitions are angering Celestine.

MARCH

Etta goes to be sterilised but is told she is already pregnant. When tests show the baby has sickle-cell anaemia, she has an abortion, which upsets her deeply religious husband. Rachel Kominsky buys 55 Victoria Road. Mark gets angry at AIDS counselling. Ian plots to evict the tramps at the Dagmar so he can have the building for his office.

APRIL

Eddie flirts with Sharon, and Grant reacts by savagely

beating Eddie, who needs brain surgery after the assault.
When he comes to he proposes to Eibhlín. Peggy Mitchell
comes to the Square to sort out her youngest, Samantha,
who has been kipping in the Arches. Arthur spots a rare
stamp on one of Sharon's letters and it ends up on *Blue
Peter*!

MAY

A shaken Eddie hides upstairs while the customers get
unruly in the bar. Ian tries to sell the café to Kath, Pauline
and Frank and tries to make them outbid each other. In
the end they buy a third each. Ricky and Sam become
engaged on her sixteenth birthday. Mark's ex-girlfriend
Gill Robinson pays him a visit.

JUNE

Nick Cotton resurfaces and this time he's back on heroin.
Ricky and Sam plot their elopement, and after she finishes
her exams, she disguises herself in a black wig and escapes
to Ricky's van and they make their way to Gretna Green.

JULY

The Mitchells and the Butchers fail to stop Ricky and
Sam getting married on the 4th. Eddie sacks Sharon for
agreeing to marry Grant and declares his intention to
rename the pub the Victoria Tavern. Dot hears that
Charlie's lorry has crashed and her husband has been
killed. A drunk Michelle ends up in bed with Clyde.

AUGUST

Rachel is after Mark but he's spending so much time with
Ian's new chef Joe that she thinks he might be gay. The

Mitchells are rigging the betting at Clyde's boxing bouts. Sharon wins her industrial tribunal for unfair dismissal but Eddie still won't reinstate her.

SEPTEMBER

Rachel and Mark sleep together and he then tells her he is HIV positive. Pete and Dot lock Nick in his bedroom in an effort to make him beat his heroin addiction. They do not notice he has a knife and can loosen the bolts on the windows. Grant and Clyde argue with Eddie because he grassed about the fixed fights, so when Eddie is murdered on the 10th they are the prime suspects.

OCTOBER

Clyde's picture is on the front page of the *Gazette* and he goes on the run, believing the police are waging a racist investigation to frame him for Eddie's murder. Michelle starts her degree at the Greater London Polytechnic. Clyde tells Michelle he wants to flee the UK with Kofi; she says she and Vicki will join them.

NOVEMBER

Clyde is in hiding at Rachel's, much to her disgust. Mark seeks out Joe who may have been a witness to the murder. Scared he will implicate Michelle, Clyde leaves Walford.

DECEMBER

Dot elicits a confession to the murder from Nick and promptly calls the police. Clyde is let off the hook and returns to Albert Square. Grant is up to something and on Boxing Day he reveals he has been planning a wedding. Sharon accepts his proposal. The Fowlers are in shock when Mark tells his parents he is HIV positive.

1992

JANUARY

Out of the blue, Willmott-Brown comes back, intent on buying a home in the Square and making Kathy fall in love with him. Pete promises to protect her. Arthur finds Mark's news hard to take and out of ignorance avoids his son. Pete organises a lynch mob for Willmott-Brown.

FEBRUARY

Grant tells Sharon he wants a baby as soon as possible; she is too scared of him to tell him she doesn't. Kathy and Pete have a showdown with James and he agrees to leave Walford – for good. Gill comes back and this time she is ill. Michelle puts two and two together and guesses that her brother is HIV positive. Ricky and Sam move into the squat. Ian tries to kiss Hattie.

MARCH

Phil meets Anne and falls in love. A few weeks later he finds out she's married and he is broken-hearted. Pauline encourages Arthur to accept Mark: he can't until Gill explains a few things. Pat's friend Lorraine dumps Mandy on the Butchers.

APRIL

Grant is behaving badly, drinking late and being obnoxious to Sharon. Lloyd is caught joy-riding. Sam wins a beauty contest at the Vic and sets her heart on a modelling career. Mrs Hewitt – a client of Arthur's – asks him to give her son a job.

MAY

Rachel loses her lecturer's job and takes shifts at the café. Ethel has her dog Willy put down. A hardened Ian hires an escort, Debbie, for a business dinner but misinterprets her professionalism as personal interest. Her rejection sends him cruising in red-light districts.

JUNE

Ricky finds Sam on a modelling job in a shopping arcade dressed as a giant Edam. Gill is so weak she is moved into a hospice. On the 11th, Phil stands in for Grant as the getaway driver on a bank raid that goes wrong. Mark arranges a wedding for him and Gill only to watch his bride die the following day on the 25th.

JULY

Sam makes it quite clear she's gone off Ricky, who is doing his best to save his marriage. Rachel starts a bric-à-brac stall and Pat starts up PatCabs.

AUGUST

Pete gives Mandy a job on the stall. She thanks him by stealing from him. When Grant doesn't come home on the 6th, Phil and Sharon steal the moment to make love. In Pauline's absence, the Square is suspicious that Arthur is having an affair with Christine Hewitt, but their relationship is platonic. Ian has a fling with an older woman, Ronnie.

SEPTEMBER

When Sharon says that she won't have Grant's baby, he responds by saying he'll sell the Vic from under her. Tricky Dicky and Rachel end up in bed together. Ian's got cockroaches *à la carte* in his kitchens, and Pauline returns from New Zealand.

OCTOBER

The organisers of a bank robbery, which Grant had supplied the driver for, demand he comes up with the £22,000 that the driver made off with. Grant sets fire to the Vic hoping to claim the insurance money to pay the thugs, but he is unaware that Sharon is upstairs crying after rowing with Phil. Ian tracks down Cindy.

NOVEMBER

On the 10th, Michelle and Sharon have a girls' night out at 'Chelle's college. Clyde and Grant follow expecting to find Sharon with another fella. They get a shock when they find Michelle in bed with another student, Jack Woodman. Out of spite, Grant tells Sharon he torched the Vic and she says she hates him. The Vic reopens on the 24th.

DECEMBER

Ian invites Cindy and Steven to spend Christmas with him. Tricky Dicky wins a holiday to Tenerife and asks Kathy to join him. Frank gets a call to say his mum has died, but before he gets a chance to grieve, Pat is arrested for drunk driving after running down and killing a girl on Christmas Eve. Jack strangely visits Michelle on Christmas Day to give her a rose. Arthur is elsewhere – at Mrs Hewitt's where he is committing adultery for the first time. On New Year's Eve, Hattie proposes to Steve and Cindy moves back in with Ian.

1993

JANUARY

Nick's trial for Eddie's murder takes place but even Dot's
emotional evidence is not enough to convict him. Pat,
ashamed, is hiding from the Square. Sam goes away for
the weekend with her upper-crust new 'friend' Clive.
Budding footballer Aidan moves in with the Fowlers. Pete
and Pauline meet Rose Chapman at a Danny Taurus pub
gig, and Pete is smitten with her.

FEBRUARY

Sam leaves Ricky and gets a job on a cruise ship. Sanjay
– an old mate of Richard's – gets Rachel's pitch. She
makes some money by tutoring Jack. Pat is up in court
but the real trial comes when she is visited by the dead
girl's mother. Kathy opens up the bistro. Sanjay loses the
deposit for his flat to Nigel in a poker game as his pregnant
wife Gita turns up.

MARCH

Rachel gets a job in Leeds and leaves Walford. On the
4th, Vicki goes missing from school. Michelle believes
unstable Jack has kidnapped her. She is found two days
later safe and well. Sharmilla is born to Sanjay and Gita
on the 18th. Rose and Pete try to stay together in the face
of threats from her gangster in-laws. On the 25th, Grant

hits a policeman investigating a report of domestic violence and is held on remand.

APRIL

With Grant behind bars. Sharon and Phil live as man and wife but things do not go well between them. Michelle asks Phil and some mates to see to Jack who is still pestering her. Danny Taurus plays at the Vic and asks Pauline to run away with him. Aidan injures his knee and is forced to give up soccer.

MAY

Aidan takes Ecstasy at a rave and collapses, ending up in hospital. He decides to return to Ireland and Mandy follows him. Pete and Rose run away together to avoid the menacing Chapmans. A long-lost relative of the Taverniers, Gidea, turns up and Clyde falls for her.

JUNE

Greg Hewitt tries to get back together with his wife, but she stands her ground and he goes away again. Nigel meets Debbie at a party. Steve runs away from the ties of Albert Square leaving Hattie a note. Phil gives her a lift to Southampton (where Steve has a job on a cruise ship) but she does not tell Steve that she is pregnant. Phil meets Nadia, an illegal immigrant from Romania, and offers to marry her.

JULY

Hattie decides to have an abortion. She changes her mind only to miscarry. On the 8th Phil and Nadia say 'I do'.

Kathy forces Christine to confess about her affair with Arthur. Clyde and Gidea leave to live in the Caribbean with Kofi. On the 27th, Dot is suspicious of Zoe who claims to be the mother of her grandson.

AUGUST

Michelle flips when she finds Shelley smoking dope with Clem and Russell when she is babysitting Vicki. Pat is released from prison on the 24th. Zoe and Ashley ask Dot to go and live with them and on the 26th, she does after Dr Legg and Ethel come round to say goodbye. On the 31st, Grant and Sharon, Pat and Frank, and Phil and Kathy go to Paris where Phil and Kathy get it together. Frank finds Diane eight months' pregnant.

SEPTEMBER

Mrs Hewitt gives Arthur an ultimatum and on the 9th, he tells Pauline he has been having an affair. She bloodies his nose with a frying pan and throws him out. Richard stirs up trouble by falsely claiming to be the father of Cindy's twins. Debbie returns and Nigel is ecstatic – until Liam beats him up the next day.

OCTOBER

By the close of play on the 5th, the whole Square knows the truth about Den and Michelle – at last. Shelley decides to teach the smug Richard a lesson by flirting with him. Janine returns to Frank's and it is clear she is unhappy.

NOVEMBER

Arthur has returned to the Square after his self-imposed exile, but Pauline won't talk to him. She goes on holiday and leaves him minding Martin. Clem, Shelley, Mark and Michelle go to Amsterdam for the weekend where Mark tells Shelley he is HIV positive. It becomes clear that Janine is being bullied at school. Nadia returns out of the blue – Kathy is upset because Phil hadn't even told her he was married!

DECEMBER

Cindy gives birth to the twins on the 9th – the same day Pete and Rose are killed in a car crash. Frank closes F&P Cabs after a sabotage campaign by a rival cab firm. Mandy and Aidan are homeless at Christmas, and he attempts suicide. Pauline lets Arthur move back into number 45, but it's separate bedrooms. On Christmas Day, Phil drunkenly sleeps with Nadia.

Roll Call

JOHN ALTMAN (NICK COTTON)
1985–1993

Thankfully, for the rest of the cast, John shares very little with screen baddie Nick and is amazed at the depths Nick has sunk to.

As he played a recurring character, John was able to pursue other projects and often pops up in guest roles on TV. John – who is married to actress and model Brigitte Poodhun – is a talented guitarist, and as well as writing songs has also written a screenplay for a road movie. He is a devoted dad to seven-year-old Rosanna.

HOWARD ANTHONY (ALAN JACKSON)
1993–PRESENT DAY

Alan Jackson is Howard's first TV role after a successful career in theatre. He has also appeared in Stanley Kubrick's Vietnam film *Full Metal Jacket*. Howard, who lives in London, is a trained marksman, and his gun skills combined with his green belt in karate means you wouldn't want to pick a fight with him! Howard is a sports fanatic and enjoys athletics, football, and cricket. He's also a skilled drummer.

KATHRYN APANOWICZ (MAGDA CZAJKOWSKI)
1987–1988

By the time Kathryn appeared in *EastEnders*, she was already well known for her portrayal of hard-nosed Nurse Rose Butchins in *Angels*, in which she co-starred with future *EastEnders* Judith Jacob and Shirley Cheriton. But even before her days in *Angels*, Kathryn had made several TV appearances as a child. At the age of nine she presented kids' show *Junior Showtime*, and continued to do so for four years. She also appeared in Alan Parker's kids' film, *Bugsy Malone*, with Jodie Foster and Scott Baio.

Like Mags, Kathryn is also half Polish, but as a native of Yorkshire her accent as Albert Square's Yorkshire Pudding (as Angie called her) was entirely genuine.

Kathryn is now a regular daytime presenter on Wire TV, the cable channel.

NICOLE ARUMUGAM (SHELLEY LEWIS)
1992–PRESENT DAY

Nicole first appeared in *EastEnders* in the classic episodes in November 1992 filmed at Michelle's college. The producers were so impressed with her scene giving Grant a dressing down that they offered a permanent role! So, just a few months after finishing drama college, she was working on the biggest show on telly! Nicole – who is half Irish and half Malaysian – commutes to the London studios from Bristol so she can still see her boyfriend. Most of the cast think Nicole is totally loopy – and she doesn't deny it!

NICK BERRY (SIMON WICKS)
1985–1990

Nick survived a near-fatal car accident when he was 21 with no permanent damage to the face that adorned the walls of thousands of teenage girls in the mid-eighties. He was very lucky – after being thrown through the windscreen and fracturing his skull it could have been a very different story.

He was offered the role of Wicksy almost before he had finished auditioning, and his is reckoned to be the fastest bit of casting in *EastEnders* history. In 1986 he was voted the sexiest man on telly, the same year his single (taken from the soap) 'Every Loser Wins' was the UK's highest-selling record and was at Number One for three weeks.

Since leaving *EastEnders*, his success in acting and music has continued, most notably with the Number Two hit *Heartbeat*, the theme tune to his popular police series of the same name. He also made an exercise video called *Nick Berry's Physical Pursuit*!

Nick has been engaged to model Rachel Robertson for years (they have never quite got round to tying the knot), and once dated Gillian Taylforth.

SUDHA BHUCHAR (MEENA MACKENZIE)
1993–PRESENT DAY

Sudha is a well-respected actress and presenter on the Asian arts scene in Britain. A talented linguist, Sudha is fluent in Urdu, Punjabi and Hindi, as well as being pretty good at Gujerati.

Before landing the part of scheming Meena, Sudha was already familiar to TV audiences through her portrayal of ambitious Kiran Bedi in *Family Pride* (where she worked with future *EastEnders* co-star Shobu Kapoor), as well as guest appearances in shows such as *Lovejoy*, *Boon* and *The Bill*.

She also presented the Asian interest shows *East* and *Network East*, and appeared as a semi-regular character, Usha Gupta, in *The Archers* on BBC radio.

HALUK BILGINER (MEHMET OSMAN)
1985–1989

Turkish-born Haluk came to Britain in the mid-seventies after doing his national service for Turkey. He made use of his rich singing voice by becoming the battalion singer!

Haluk nearly landed the role of Ali, but the producers thought he looked too tough, and as Ali was meant to be a bit henpecked, they created the role of Mehmet (the Terrible Turk) for Haluk, a part which brought the actor sackfuls of fan mail from adoring female admirers.

After leaving *EastEnders* in 1989, Haluk made use of his voice by appearing in stage musicals before returning to Turkey, where he lives with his wife and runs a theatre company.

PAUL BRADLEY (NIGEL BATES)
1992–PRESENT DAY

Nigel is often Albert Square's figure of fun, and Paul is no stranger to making people laugh. He is a talented comic and made his early TV appearances in *The Young Ones* and *Bottom*.

He also fronts a cabaret band called the hKippers ('Because there's never been a silent "h" in the English language before') in which he plays a guitar, nasal flute(!) and the dramnonie (an instrument Paul invented from a piece of gas piping and a clarinet reed).

He lives with his girlfriend Lynn, and they have a three-year-old son Matty and a one-year-old daughter, Maude, who attend the crèche at the *EastEnders* studio.

JUNE BROWN (DOT COTTON)
1985–1993

Like Dot, June Brown is no stranger to tragedy. As a child she lost both a brother and a sister before she was six. And by the time she had joined the Wrens in the Second World War, she had also lost her father to alcoholism and her mother to cancer.

She met her first husband at the Old Vic Theatre school (with whom she toured Europe for seven years), but the marriage ended in tragedy when June returned home to find her husband had killed himself because he thought he was terminally ill.

June later married actor Robert Arnold and they live in Croydon with assorted cats and dogs. Although June once suffered the agony of losing a premature baby, she now has five grown-up children who have provided her with grandchildren to keep her busy.

Since leaving *EastEnders* in June 1993, June has produced, directed and starred in a play called *Double D* at the Edinburgh Festival which transferred to London. She became a pop star to her amusement when she recorded her own version of 'Little Donkey' to raise funds for a donkey sanctuary in Buxton.

TODD CARTY (MARK FOWLER)
1990–PRESENT DAY

Todd took over the role of Mark in 1990 following the suicide of the actor who originally played him, David Scarboro. Todd was already a familiar face to viewers as the cheeky scallywag Tucker Jenkins in *Grange Hill*. Todd graduated from *Grange Hill* with his own spin-off show, *Tucker's Luck*, and has effectively grown up on screen.

Todd shares Mark's fascination with motorbikes and his pride and joy is a Honda 850cc, although he uses a car to get to the studio from his North London home and back. Even an accident when he was seventeen in which he smashed all the bones in his left hand couldn't put him off – he was more worried about his bike than himself!

Like Mark, Todd also comes from a supportive family who – along with his girlfriend – offered comfort when he was filming Gill's harrowing death scenes. Todd has received much praise for his portrayal of HIV-infected Mark, and he consulted the Terrence Higgins Trust to make sure his portrayal is believable.

MICHAEL CASHMAN (COLIN RUSSELL)
1986–1989

When Colin left Albert Square to live with his brother in Bristol, Michael went straight into a tour of an Agatha

Christie play, and has been working consistently in theatre ever since.

Michael became a spokesman for gay rights in Britain after a national newspaper printed his full address, leading to homophobic vandalism of his house in the East End.

He has made documentaries for the BBC about the outrage caused by Colin's screen kiss with boyfriend Barry (Gary Hailes) in an attempt to break down mistrust and homophobia.

Along with co-star Pam St Clement, Michael became one of the directors of the gay rights charity Stonewall, and continues to speak out on gay rights issues.

SHIRLEY CHERITON (DEBBIE WILKINS) 1985–1987

Debs left the Square to marry Detective Sergeant Terry Rich, played by Gary Whelan, who coincidentally had already married Shirley on screen when she played a nurse in *Angels*!

Shirley fell in love with Ross Davidson who played Debbie's lover Andy and she left her husband (with whom she has a thirteen-year-old son, Mark) to live with Ross.

Shirley and Ross have since split up, and Shirley now lives on the outskirts of London with her son. Work since *EastEnders* includes appearances in *Grace and Favour* and *Three Up, Two Down*, as well as numerous stage shows and corporate videos.

MICHELLE COLLINS (CINDY BEALE) 1988–1990, 1992–PRESENT DAY

Michelle studied drama at Kingsway College where she got to know fellow student Steve McFadden (Phil Mitchell), who was on a social science course, and the two often went on double dates with their respective partners.

Michelle was originally offered the role of Cindy for

222

eleven episodes, but ended up staying for two and a half years, before leaving for eighteen months to present the Channel 4 youth programme, *The Word*. Michelle also started to record a debut album (she had previously been a backing singer for Mari Wilson), but when she was approached by the *EastEnders* producers in March 1992 to return to the show, her album had to be put on hold, although she did release a cover version of the Temptations hit 'Get Ready'.

Michelle lives in Fulham but her fiancé of several years, Nick Fordyce, lives in Spain where he owns a nightclub. Michelle and her sister Vicky are very close to their mum, who brought them up single-handedly after a split from Michelle's dad.

LINDSEY COULSON (CAROL JACKSON)
1993–PRESENT DAY

Carol is Lindsey's first major TV role, although she has made guest appearances in shows such as *The Bill*. Lindsey claims to be one of the scruffiest people in the world and has contemplated dressing up to go to Sainsbury's so she doesn't get recognised! She is married to her agent, Philip Chard, and they have a two-year-old daughter, Molly Claire. Lindsey is an ardent supporter of Greenpeace and has campaigned for them in the past. A fan of natural medicine, she preferred to spend her eighteen-hour labour in a birthing pool rather than take pain-killers. 'At the end of it I looked like a prune, I'd been in the water for so long!'

LINDA DAVIDSON (MARY SMITH)
1985–1988

One-time partner of Nejdet Salih, Linda later married TV floor manager Robin Greene. She has worked in theatre, avoiding comparisons with the troubled punk that made her famous, and has occasionally popped up on TV in guest roles in shows like *The Last of the Summer Wine*.

ROSS DAVIDSON (ANDY O'BRIEN)
1985–1986

Like many other soap stars, Ross too made the crossover into presenting and was a regular host on *Daytime Live*, Sky TV and *Run the Gauntlet*.

Ross left *EastEnders* in a blaze of publicity – he was the first character to be killed off in the soap – and he hoped to become the next James Bond. At the time he was dating Andy's screen lover, Shirley Cheriton, who played Debbie.

Before deciding to become an actor, Scots-born Ross qualified as a PE teacher and taught in schools for two years. He is still a keep-fit fanatic and enjoys everything from water-polo to horse riding.

SUSANNAH DAWSON (GILL FOWLER)
1991–1992

Sue was only in *EastEnders* for a year, but in that time she made her mark in the public eye, playing AIDS patient Gill Fowler.

Following the screening of the episode of Gill's death (which was watched by 20 million people), Sue was inundated with letters from fans. She was so stunned by the reaction that she decided to use her notoriety as Gill to promote AIDS awareness, hoping to reach the ignorant people who had mixed fact and fiction and had abused her in the street when she was on screen.

Susannah wrote a book, specifically for kids, called *Gill and Mark, EastEnders' Great Love Story*, and produced the accompanying video.

She lives in North London with her son, Joe.

LETITIA DEAN (SHARON MITCHELL)
1985–PRESENT DAY

When Letitia got the role of Sharon straight from school, she thought it would only last for six weeks, but she's stayed in Albert Square for nine years and is one of only six remaining cast members.

Julia Smith gave Tish the role because she had the dirtiest laugh she'd ever heard, which, combined with her angelic looks, made her perfect to play confused Sharon. In the early days of the show it was actually in Tish's contract that she couldn't lose any weight!

When *EastEnders* was keeping tabloid journalists in business in the mid-eighties, Letitia was crushed by the kiss-and-tell sensations of an ex-boyfriend, and the publication of a doctored 'glamour' photo that had her head superimposed on to the body of another woman. Consequently, Letitia became cagey about talking about her romantic life, but when she started dating BBC production worker Neil McLintock in 1992, she was sure enough of love to go public with their romance.

Tish got a chance to show off her singing voice, when storylines had Sharon singing with The Banned. A natural spin-off from this was the release of the single 'Something Outta Nothing' with Paul J. Medford, which enjoyed limited chart success.

Every Christmas, Letitia flexes her vocal chords when she does panto. As a kid, she won talent contests singing with her older brother Stephen, with whom she now shares a flat in the West End of London.

She is great friends with Susan Tully, who plays Sharon's best mate Michelle, and the two are often seen gossiping in their shared dressing room when not recording.

PETER DEAN (PETE BEALE)
1985–1993

Peter is a genuine Cockney. He comes from a family of market traders and his childhood mates included the Kray twins.

As a lad he worked on a fruit and veg stall in Chapel Market in North London, so when he landed the role of stall-holder Pete Beale he didn't need to be told how to look natural!

Peter was 29 when he first met his second wife Jean (his first marriage ended after three years and one daughter, Leah) when Jean was just fifteen and babysitting for a friend. They live above a café on East End Road and do not have any children. They would have liked to adopt, but a teenage conviction of Peter's meant they were ineligible. Peter and Jean are both practising Buddhists (that's why Pete was always seen drinking from a pewter tankard, because Peter didn't drink beer).

Peter's contract with *EastEnders* was terminated in the spring of 1993, and on leaving the show Peter told all to the *Sun* newspaper about his suspicions of earlier plans to write him out of Albert Square, as well as his feelings about former co-stars.

Since leaving, he has toured in the play *Entertaining Mr Sloane* and appeared in panto.

ANITA DOBSON (ANGIE WATTS)
1985–1988

Born just off the Mile End Road, Anita is another of the cast's genuine East Enders. Her wonderful performance as Angie was integral to the show's early success, but even though Anita is still one of Britain's most popular actresses, she has been unable to repeat that success.

Her West End musical *Budgie*, with Adam Faith, had only a short run. *Split Ends*, her very own sitcom set in a hairdresser's, failed to connect with viewers and ran for only one series.

Anita got excellent reviews for the musical *Rough Crossing*, and even better ones for *My Lovely . . . Shayna Maidel*, in which she played a Holocaust survivor. Unfortunately, her next West End foray was less successful: *Eurovision*, a camp musical comedy, lasted only five nights.

She has recorded two albums and her single, 'Anyone Can Fall in Love' (based on the *EastEnders* theme tune), was a hit in 1987.

Anita lives with former Queen guitarist Brian May.

NICOLA DUFFETT (DEBBIE TYLER)
1993–PRESENT DAY

Single mum Nicola first made her name in the Oscar-winning film *Howard's End* playing the prostitute, Jackie Bast.

Nicola had already made several TV appearances in *The Bill* and *Maigret*, as well as providing one of the voices for cult sci-fi show *Jupiter Moon*.

Before joining *EastEnders*, Nicola was a genuine fan of the show, and rates Bill Treacher's performance during Arthur's breakdown as 'the greatest piece of television acting I've ever seen'.

TOMMY EYTLE (JULES TAVERNIER)
1990–PRESENT DAY

Born in Guyana, Tommy came to Britain for a holiday in 1951 and stayed!

His varied career includes stints as a surveyor and draughtsman, as well as a band leader.

Tommy, who lives in Surrey, reckons he's a lot like the character he plays – he likes a chat and an easy life, and can be relied upon in a crisis.

LEONARD FENTON (DR HAROLD LEGG)
1985–PRESENT DAY

Born in the East End, Leonard qualified as a civil engineer before deciding he wanted to be an actor. He paid for his acting tuition by teaching mathematics at Westminster Polytechnic.

As he plays a recurring character, Leonard has plenty of opportunity to take roles on TV and in the theatre. He lives in London with his wife, cellist Madeleine Thorner, with whom he has four children.

Leonard is a talented painter, and has had several exhibitions of his work. Another little-known fact about Leonard is that he is a talented dog impressionist!

GRETCHEN FRANKLIN (ETHEL SKINNER)
1985–PRESENT DAY

Like her friend Leonard Fenton, Gretchen is another of the Albert Square semi-regulars.

Gretchen started off in showbusiness as a showgirl and dancer, and was the toast of the town with her good looks and sense of humour. She certainly won the heart of the writer Caswell Garth who married her!

Although it took the part of scatty Ethel to make her loved by the public, it could have happened much earlier if she'd accepted the role of Alf Garnet's missus in *Till Death Do Us Part*, the role she created on stage.

Gretchen is a devoted animal lover, and would have loved to have taken Ethel's pug dog Willy home with her. She lives in Richmond where she is president of the local RSPCA.

DEAN GAFFNEY (ROBBIE JACKSON)
1993–PRESENT DAY

At sixteen, Dean is already an accomplished veteran of film (he was in *The Power of One* with Stephen Dorff), theatre (*Waiting for Godot*) and TV (he has had roles in *The Bill* and kids' drama *Oasis*).

Dean is a passionate supporter of his local football team, Brentford FC. He has one older brother and lives with his family in West London. He was inspired to go into acting after seeing a Michael J. Fox film, and says the actor he most admires is David Jason.

MICHELLE GAYLE (HATTIE TAVERNIER)
1990–1993

Like many of her co-stars, Michelle has also recorded an album, but unlike most of the other East Enders' efforts, Michelle looks set to have a serious second career in music.

After proving herself as an actress with Hattie's heart-breaking miscarriage, Michelle launched into the pop world in July 1993 with the chart success 'Looking Up'.

Another similarity Michelle shares with several other East Enders is the fact that she started her TV career on *Grange Hill*, playing Fiona Wilson. During her time with the show, Michelle used to drive around the back lot from her dressing room to the set to the canteen – even though all these places are just a couple of hundred yards from each other!

Twenty-three-year-old Michelle lives in Harlesden, North London, with her dog, Rude Boy.

SHREELA GHOSTH (NAIMA JEFFREY)
1985–1987

During her time with *EastEnders*, Shreela – along with co-star Paul J. Medford – opened a wine bar called Cobblers in Bethnal Green in the real East End. She also had a whirlwind romance with film director Jonathan Curling during her first few months in Albert Square, and soon took a few months' maternity leave to have her first child.

Shreela's credits include *The Chinese Detective* and *The Jewel in the Crown*. She has since left acting to become a journalist, and at one point was a reporter for the regional news show, *Newsroom South East*.

LESLIE GRANTHAM (DEN WATTS)
1985–1989

Leslie left school at fifteen, and after a few dead-end jobs enlisted in the army, and at the age of nineteen was posted to the Royal Fusiliers in Germany. In 1966 he was convicted of the manslaughter of a taxi driver in Germany and served eleven years in prison for the crime.

The *Sun* newspaper broke the story three days after *EastEnders* started, and Leslie quickly became the target of tabloid obsession and at times needed more security to sneak him into the studios than the Princess of Wales when she visited Albert Square! His notoriety meant that his personal life – the birth of his first son Spike and the death of his brother Philip from AIDS – became front-page news.

It was during his sentence at Wormwood Scrubs that Leslie caught the acting bug when he saw an amateur show and realised he could do it better! On his release, Leslie studied acting and paid his way through college by taking a job painting the VD clinic at St Thomas's Hospital.

When the word went out about the auditions for *EastEnders*, Leslie thought he would try for the role of Pete Beale, but was offered the part of Den, which at the time was envisaged to be a minor part. But Leslie's portrayal of the lecherous landlord was so good that he quickly became one of the most popular actors in the country.

It was at Leslie's request that Den was killed off, and he was disappointed that the scenes he filmed of Den's lifeless body in the murky waters of the canal weren't shown, leaving the viewers thinking that Den may, one day, return. Leslie himself has ruled out such a comeback.

Since leaving *EastEnders*, Leslie has appeared regularly on TV in *Winners and Losers*, *The Paradise Club*, *Cluedo*, and most recently as undercover cop Mick Raynor in *99–1*, a show written specially for him.

Leslie also ventured into the West End for the first time with a production of *Rick's Café Casablanca*, although it wasn't the success everyone had hoped for.

Leslie is married to actress Jane Laurie, with whom he has two sons.

KEITH HARRIS (DESIGNER) 1985–1990

Keith's input was arguably as important as the contributions made by Tony Holland and Julia Smith towards the huge success of *EastEnders*.

Along with his team of professionals, Keith created the most realistic set British television had ever known – so realistic, in fact, that many people thought Albert Square was a real place!

Keith made several trips to the East End taking photos and making detailed sketches of old buildings to make Albert Square as authentic as possible.

His attention to detail was so complete that when builders made a garden wall too straight, he ordered the wall to be dismantled and rebuilt crooked!

Keith stayed with *EastEnders* for a further five years, and after leaving took on the task of creating the marvellous Los Barcos set for *Eldorado*, arguably the most competent contribution anyone made to the doomed sunsoap.

Keith's other credits include the sets for Miss World and Miss UK contests, as well as the stage for the BAFTA awards.

TONY HOLLAND (CO-CREATOR & ORIGINAL STORYLINER)

As he comes from a traditional East End family, Tony was able to create the Beales and the Fowlers from his personal memories.

Like Albert Beale, Tony's father was a soldier, and Tony followed in the family tradition for a while before becoming an actor, and then a writer. It was while he was script-editing *Z Cars* that he first met his *EastEnders* collaborator, Julia Smith.

He worked for Thames Television for years on shows such as *Marked Personal*, the short-lived daytime soap *Rooms*, and *The Life and Death of Penelope*.

After a stint as a script editor with BBC radio, he worked on three shows with Julia: *Angels*, *The District Nurse* and *Cold Warrior*, before they created *EastEnders*.

When the BBC wanted to make a three-times-a-week soap in the early nineties, they turned to Tony to come up with the formula for *Eldorado*. However, even Tony's wealth of experience in TV couldn't help *Eldorado* emulate the success of her older sister, *EastEnders*.

JUDITH JACOB (CARMEL ROBERTS)
1986–1989

Like Shirley Cheriton, Kathryn Apanowicz, Julia Smith and Tony Holland, Judith was also a graduate of *Angels*, the drama in which she played Nurse Beverley Slater.

Judith, whose daughter Aisha played Carmel's niece in *EastEnders*, can still be seen on TV in the comedy sketch show *The Real McCoy*. She has also formed the BiBi Crew Theatre Company with six other actors, who produce and tour their own productions.

OSCAR JAMES (TONY CARPENTER)
1985–1987

Oscar left his native Trinidad when he was fourteen by running off to sea. He travelled the world before settling in London. Before landing the part of Tony, Oscar had worked steadily in TV in shows such as *Angels* and *Emmerdale*. He is a gifted comedian and singer (he too released a single while he was with *EastEnders*), and since leaving Albert Square he has worked steadily in musicals and comedies in theatre. He has also been in Shakespeare productions at the National Theatre.

Tony is a single parent who has two daughters and lives in London.

ANDREW JOHNSON (SAEED JEFFREY)
1985–1986

Since leaving *EastEnders*, Andrew has changed his name to Andrew Johnson-Brye because there was already another Andrew Johnson on the Equity register in America, where he went to find work.

He has been seen in the films *Rider on the Storm* and *A Kind of English*, as well as making several appearances on Angela Lansbury's TV show, *Murder She Wrote*.

SHOBU KAPOOR (GITA KAPOOR)
1993–PRESENT DAY

Shobu is the shortest member of *EastEnders*' adult cast, at just 4'10". She first worked with Sudha Bhuchar, who plays her cheating sister Meena, on the Central TV Asian soap, *Family Pride*. She played Nasreen Ali, who was in a constant state of mental breakdown after a disastrous marriage, proving Shobu's ability for nerve-wracking drama. Shobu has also worked in theatre, appearing at the Bristol Old Vic and Theatre Royal, Stratford, and has played in various radio productions.

ELIZABETH KELLY (NELLIE ELLIS)
1993–PRESENT DAY

Elizabeth was born in Newcastle but has adopted Yorkshire as her home. A widow, she has one daughter and one son (who live in France and Spain), two grandchildren and one great-granddaughter, Sophie, whom she adores.

Elizabeth had previously had a small role in *Coronation Street*, and has appeared in several of the UK's most popular shows. She was a fan of *EastEnders* before joining the cast in late 1993 – it was in fact the only soap she watched.

ROSS KEMP (GRANT MITCHELL)
1990–PRESENT DAY

Sports fanatic Ross claims he's a real softie compared to hot-headed Grant. 'I didn't even smoke my first cigarette until I was 23,' he has said.

Ross, 29, is a native of Brentwood, Essex, where he still plays for his old rugby club. In 1993, Ross trained for and completed the London Marathon, raising thousands of pounds for a medical research charity. He lives with his journalist girlfriend Sue, and he says at some point in the future he would like to have kids and get married.

SOPHIE LAWRENCE (DIANE BUTCHER)
1988–1991, AUGUST 1993

When Sophie left *EastEnders* in 1991 she released a single, 'Love's Unkind', which got to Number 21 in the charts. Sadly, her follow-up single, 'Secrets', failed to enter the Top 40.

Sophie had always hoped to combine both singing and acting, but success has eluded her in both disciplines since leaving Walford. She co-owns a baby-wear shop in Epping called No Ribbons for Harry, and although she regularly appears in theatre, her only return to TV was her brief reappearance in *EastEnders* when Frank tracked Diane down in Paris.

Money worries affected Sophie in 1993 when she had a dispute with her agent of the time over payments from radio and theatre performances.

During her time with the show, Sophie had a well-publicised affair with BBC kids'-TV presenter, Simon Parkin.

SEAN MAGUIRE (AIDAN BROSNAN)
1993

Sean is another of the East Enders who cut their teeth on *Grange Hill*. He played cute tearaway Tegs for three years before graduating to the neighbouring set of *EastEnders*.

Playing Irish Aidan was easy for Sean, whose parents are both Irish – he didn't have any problems with the accent! Sean was taken aback by the attention he got from teenage girls and teen magazines, as he quickly became one of the most popular faces on TV.

His close relationship with co-star Nicola Stapleton sparked incorrect rumours that the two were an item. While he was still in the show he formed the group Back Up with his brother and two cousins; he also developed a taste for the dangerous sport speedway which led to an accident where he smashed his ankle and was in a full-length cast for months.

His accident meant a hasty rewrite of key Christmas episodes to explain his absence, as well as lots of extra work for his colleagues.

Sean recovered from his break to pursue a future with Back Up after leaving the soap.

JACQUETTA MAY (RACHEL KOMINSKY)
1991–1993

Born in Kent and trained at Birmingham University, Jacquetta had a successful career in theatre (including plays at the National Theatre) before joining the *East-Enders* cast in 1991.

She described herself as pretty similar to her on-screen character of university lecturer Rachel, although she says she's not quite as earnest – in fact Jacquetta has quite a wicked sense of humour!

Life after *EastEnders* has included occasional TV appearances, including *In Suspicious Circumstances*, and a successful return to the theatre.

STEVE MCFADDEN (PHIL MITCHELL)
1990–PRESENT DAY

One of the most secretive members of the cast, Steve has a policy of not giving interviews to the press. Before training at RADA to be an actor, he studied to be a social worker. Steve, who has a son, Matthew, by his childhood sweetheart, lives in Tufnell Park, North London, and enjoys karate, boxing, snooker and sailing. He has trained in stage fighting – so that's why Phil's on-screen bust-ups always look so convincing!

MICHAEL MELIA (EDDIE ROYLE)
1990–1991

Born in Berkshire, Michael originally had ambitions to be a school teacher which he fulfilled before running a bar in Spain.

He was perfect for the part of ex-copper Eddie Royle because of his boxer's looks, but Michael didn't get his knocks in the ring. He has in fact broken his nose three times, once falling off a trolley as a kid, then running into a gate and finally in a game of football.

Michael was upset when Eddie was killed off because he felt that a year hadn't been long enough to establish the character. However, he soon came to terms with the loss of a regular job and now regularly pops up in guest roles on TV.

PAUL J. MEDFORD (KELVIN CARPENTER)
1985–1987

Paul was destined to be in *EastEnders* – so many different agents sent in Paul's CV to Tony Holland and Julia Smith that they knew they had to see him for the part of Kelvin. Paul, who was born in West London, released a single with Letitia Dean called 'Something Outta Nothing' taken from their storyline, which had Kelvin and Sharon in a pop group called The Banned.

On leaving *EastEnders* in 1987, Paul set about realising his dream of becoming an English Sammy Davis Jr. A talented singer and dancer, Paul has since appeared in the West End productions of *Five Guys Named Mo* and *Hair*.

MARK MONERO (STEVE ELLIOT)
1992–PRESENT DAY

Playing laid-back Steve suits Mark down to the ground: when Steve took off to see the world on a cruise ship in 1993, Mark used his break from the show to go travelling too, and spent several months in Thailand.

Mark is a talented musician (he plays piano and drums) and would one day like to have a bash at the music industry. He's also a pretty good dancer, as he used to break-dance as a teenager.

Before *EastEnders* Mark appeared in many, many shows ranging from *The Paradise Club* to *The Firm* and

The Bill. When he finishes with *EastEnders*, he says he would like to go into theatre.

SID OWEN (RICKY BUTCHER)
1988–PRESENT DAY

Born David Owen, Sid has been acting since he was a kid and even appeared with Al Pacino in the film *Revolution*.

Sid had the misfortune to have the dressing room between good mates Danniella Westbrook and Nicola Stapleton, and had to put up with the two of them shouting to each other making arrangements to go out!

As well as being pals with those two, he also gets on well with Steve McFadden. Sid is another sporty type and enjoys skiing, football and motorbikes. He dated Nick Berry's younger sister Amanda for three years but now lives in his own bachelor pad in Wanstead.

PATSY PALMER (BIANCA JACKSON)
1993–PRESENT DAY

Patsy is a genuine East Ender and lives in a flat in Bethnal Green, although she regularly visits her mum and dad who actually live round the corner from a pub called the Queen Victoria (Patsy says she's never been in it)!

Twenty-year-old Patsy started off in TV as a regular extra in *Grange Hill*, which supplied her with pocket money while she was still in school. She was very nearly turned down for the part of Bianca because the producers thought she was too old (Bianca is six years her junior), but they were so impressed with her when a talent scout went to her drama school (which she still attends now she's working) that she was given the part anyway.

Patsy's other work includes commercials for Phileas Fogg and Clearasil.

LOUISE PLOWRIGHT (JULIE COOPER)
1989–1990

Before Louise became an actress she managed a shoe shop in Chorley, Lancashire! She very nearly lost the part of maneater Julie because the producers thought she was too young to have the necessary experience with men, but Louise soon convinced them when she did her Bette Midler impression at her audition!

Louise was only with the show for a year, and although she wouldn't have minded staying longer, she says the split was amicable. 'They just didn't know where to go with the character.'

But Louise knew where to go – back to the theatre where she made use of her singing voice in shows like *Les Miserables*. She also took on the role of feisty Linda Harvey in the daytime soap *Families* for a year.

SANDY RADCLIFFE (SUE OSMAN)
1985–1989

Sandy has worked little since her time in *EastEnders*. She has often been in the headlines of the tabloid press because of her alleged use of drugs, including heroin. She actually served time in Holloway women's prison in 1983 for conspiracy to sell cannabis, and once the papers got hold of this information, Sandy was exposed to horrific invasions of privacy. She offered to leave the soap, but producer Julia Smith stood by her, and Sandy remained for another two years. In the sixties, Sandy's stunning looks – and her enjoyment of 'Swinging London' – made her the perfect model, and she was picked by Lord Snowdon as his Face of the Seventies.

Sandy made the crossover into acting with parts in shows like *Minder*, *Shelley* and *Shoestring* before winning the role as long-suffering Sue.

She has one grown-up son, William.

IAN REDDINGTON (RICHARD COLE)
1992–1994

Sheffield-born Ian is one of the most respected actors in the cast. He had an illustrious career in theatre (he was with the RSC for a while and even played Macbeth) before switching to TV roles, including parts in *Casualty*, *The Bill* and *Inspector Morse*.

When he was offered the role of Tricky Dicky, the producers wanted their new market inspector to have a London accent and wear a uniform! But Ian soon put them right (although he would have had no problem doing the accent).

Playing a baddie has earnt him the attention of lots of adoring female fans, but he has to let them down by telling them that he's actually quite nice in real life! 'I'm much nicer than he is. I'm also more open and honest,' he has said.

He is a devoted fan of Sheffield Wednesday, and even recorded a one-off single in support of the team's assault on Wembley in 1993 called 'If it's Wednesday It Must Be Wembley'. He promises it will be his only foray into pop.

MIKE REID (FRANK BUTCHER)
1987–1994

A former coalman, Mike got his break into showbusiness at a talent contest at Butlins, Minehead. He won through to the finals at the Palladium and landed himself a part on the TV show *The Comedians*.

He met his second wife Shirley on a blind date (Mike married his first wife young and was a father at seventeen) and they have been together for over thirty years now, offering each other much-needed support during a series of family tragedies after Mike joined *EastEnders*.

First his son Mark accidentally killed his best friend and then killed himself out of guilt. Then, only months later,

Mark's daughter Kirsty died of cot death. Mike now dotes on Kirsty's twin brother Michael.

Mike has been one of *EastEnders*' great comedians and earnt a reputation for himself as something of an ad-libber! Throughout his years at *EastEnders* he maintained a second career as a stand-up comedian and cabaret artist. His live shows are pretty raunchy, but popular none the less, and Mike has made two highly successful videos of his shows. He left Albert Square in 1994 to devote more time to his comedy, but there is every chance Mike – and Frank – will return to Walford in the future.

WENDY RICHARD (PAULINE FOWLER)
1985–PRESENT DAY

Before she took the role of cardigan-clad Pauline Fowler, Wendy was well known to viewers from roles in shows like *The Newcomers*, *Z Cars* and, of course, as Miss Brahms in *Are You Being Served?*

Her successful career was sadly underscored by an unsettled private life that included a peripatetic childhood, the loss of her father at age eleven to suicide, two failed marriages and her own suicide attempt at 28 following the death of her mother.

Wendy is now married to her third husband, Paul, and although she has no children she has made up for it by earning the respect of so many of the younger cast of *EastEnders*: Susan Tully and Adam Woodyatt both treat Wendy as a confidante – Susan even calls Wendy 'Mum' occasionally!

AFTAB SACHAK (ASHRAF KARIM)
1988–1989

Born in East Africa, Aftab enjoyed something of a playboy lifestyle round London before landing the part of

Ashraf. During his run, he was reported in the press as facing bankruptcy due to large gambling debts.

Aftab still takes occasional acting parts when they become available, and has been seen in the TV comedy *Waiting for God*. Mostly, though, Aftab busies himself running a nightclub in London.

NEJDET SALIH (ALI OSMAN) 1985–1989

Nejdet was born in London but as a toddler was sent to live with relatives in Cyprus because the warmer climate helped his asthma.

Nej is therefore fluent in Turkish and when he returned to London for schooling had to learn English all over again.

During his years with *EastEnders*, Nej had a romance with Linda Davidson and formed a firm friendship with June Brown, who played Dot Cotton.

When he left Albert Square, Nejdet went in search of work in America, but returned to the UK for a part in the film *Carry on Columbus*.

He is now married to Susan, and in 1993 successfully sued a newspaper that claimed he had cheated on his wife and unfairly alleged that he was a playboy. In his own words, Nej has described himself as more of a wimp than a romeo!

JULIA SMITH (CO-CREATOR AND ORIGINAL PRODUCER) 1985–1989

Born in London, Julia trained at RADA before becoming a production assistant at the BBC. After a stint in theatre, Julia returned to the BBC as a director for shows such as *Doctor Who*, *Dr Finlay's Casebook* and *Z Cars*, where she met then script editor Tony Holland.

For nine years she produced the phenomenally successful

hospital series *Angels* before co-creating *The District Nurse* with Tony, with whom, of course, she devised *EastEnders*.

During her time as producer of *EastEnders*, the press tagged her the Godmother because of her reported dictatorial way of managing things, but she was obviously well enough liked to be asked to produce the BBC's soap for the nineties, *Eldorado*.

Julia was put under extraordinary time constraints after the launch date for the three-times-a-week soap was brought forward to July 1992, and after a few months of running the ailing production, Julia took leave as she was physically exhausted.

And anyway, her dog Roly (yes, *the* Roly) was missing her!

NICOLA STAPLETON (MANDY SALTER)
1992–1994

A very talented young actress, Nicola made teenage tearaway Mandy one of the most hated characters on television.

Nicola grew up in South London and started acting at seven when a teacher suggested it might be a good way of using up her surplus energy!

She appeared in plenty of ads, a film with Charlie Sheen, and the kids' drama *Hansel and Gretel*, before she made her name as *EastEnders*' teenager from hell.

Playing Mandy gave her a chance to work with her long-time friend, Danniella Westbrook (at one time the two pals even bought matching jeeps!), as well as get up the noses of 20 million viewers. Some viewers detested Mandy so much that Nicola was subjected to taunts in the street, and her car was regularly vandalised.

Nicola stopped filming *EastEnders* at the end of 1993 when she went to Los Angeles where, as well as getting a few offers of work, she posed for an underwear shoot with *GQ* magazine. 'But I didn't go topless because my dad would kill me!'

Even though Nicola is very much her own woman at such a young age (she is only nineteen), her dad still keeps a keen eye on her and her younger brother Vincent.

PAM ST CLEMENT (PAT BUTCHER)
1986–PRESENT DAY

Although Pam was actually born in Middlesex, she lived for a while in Stepney – well within the sound of Bow Bells. Before the acting bug got the better of her, Pam worked both as a teacher and journalist, but has since worked extensively in TV and theatre.

She is a real pet lover, and has been involved with a sanctuary for sick animals and as a kid thought she would grow up to become a vet.

In 1991 Pam, who is divorced, added her name to a list actors and actresses indentifying themselves as gay to support Ian McKellen's decision to accept his knighthood.

GILLIAN TAYLFORTH (KATHY BEALE)
1985–PRESENT DAY

More actresses were seen for the role of Kathy than any other role, even though the producers had already auditioned Gilly. The truth was they thought she was too young and too pretty to be the downtrodden wife of Pete. But Gillian's gutsiness won them over, and after a quick bit of calculation the producers decided that she was *just* old enough to be Ian's mum.

Like Kathy, Gillian also comes from a big family, to which she added her own contribution, Jessica, in January 1992. Gillian lives in North London with her partner, businessman Geoff Knights, and can often be seen buying her fruit and veg in Islington's Chapel Street market. In January 1994, she lost a high-profile libel suit against *The Sun*, and was ordered to pay £500,000 costs.

BILL TREACHER (ARTHUR FOWLER)
1985–PRESENT DAY

Bill Treacher is universally loved on the *EastEnders* set. He is highly respected as an actor (he was actually the first and only choice to play Arthur), but much of the affection is due to his talents as a comic. He regularly reduces his co-stars to fits of giggles.

Julia Smith and Tony Holland remembered Bill from his work on *Z Cars*, and asked him to play Arthur. Knowing that the part would be a huge commitment, he asked his wife Kate and children Jamie and Sophie before accepting the part.

A dedicated family man, Bill makes the trip to the London studios from his home in Suffolk to make sure he gets to see his brood.

SUSAN TULLY (MICHELLE FOWLER)
1985–PRESENT DAY

One of the most outstanding young actresses of her generation, Susan Tully quickly became a heroine to her peers when her character, Michelle, got pregnant at sixteen by her best friend's dad.

Possibly the first teen character on TV to be given a truly adult storyline, Susan evolved as one of the show's early stars and became an unofficial spokeswoman and agony aunt for teen mums throughout Britain. She made use of her presenting skills when she made a documentary about single mums called *Too Young to Have a Baby*.

Susan was already well known to fans due to her role of rebellious Suzanne Ross in *Grange Hill*. Some older viewers also remembered her as the nine-year-old presenter of the kids' programme *Our Show*.

When she was told at her audition that Michelle would soon be pregnant, Sue was relieved to know Michelle would keep the baby and give her a chance to 'grow up' on screen.

Susan is very close to Samantha Leigh Martin, who plays Michelle's daughter Vicki, and visits Samantha when she isn't filming for a couple of weeks, so that the little girl doesn't forget who her screen mum is.

Susan's London accent is entirely authentic, but that's not the only similarity she shares with her on-screen character. Like Arthur, Susan's dad was also unemployed for a long time, and like Pauline, Susan's mum also had a baby late in life, providing Susan with her little sister Linda, on whom she dotes.

Susan is great mates with Letitia Dean who plays Michelle's best friend Sharon, although the two have stopped going to the endless stream of parties and premieres that tempted them in the early days of *EastEnders*.

It's a well-known fact that Susan is an ardent fan of Arsenal football club (she even bought a flat once because it had a view over their Highbury ground), but it's not so well known that Susan also claims to be able to hum the theme tune to every show on telly!

DEEPAK VERMA (SANJAY KAPOOR)
1993–PRESENT DAY

Another East End native, Deepak lives with his family in Hackney. When he's not filming, Deepak works with his own theatre company and writes plays (in the past he has been commissioned by the Royal Court Theatre Company).

A dedicated and enthusiastic actor, Deepak can come across as being very serious (he is even teetotal) but on closer inspection he reveals a very sly sense of humour!

TOM WATT (GEORGE 'LOFTY' HOLLOWAY)
1985–1988

It came as no surprise to Tom's friends that on leaving *EastEnders* – the show that not only gave him fame but also a brief affair with Anita Dobson – the academic actor turned his hand to playwrighting and formed his own theatre company.

As well as countless stage appearances, Tom has continued to pop up on TV in shows such as *Boon* and *South of the Border*, and also a couple of pilot shows that never took off.

A dedicated fan of 'The Arsenal', Tom has written a book about football fans' lives on the terraces.

DANNIELLA WESTBROOK (SAMANTHA BUTCHER) 1990–1993

A talented singer, Danniella has always threatened to become a pop success, but her acting successes have always got in her way.

Her *EastEnders* fame brought her grief when her BMW car was broken into, but not much wipes the smile from this one's face.

Straight after leaving *EastEnders* in early 1993, Danniella started filming the drama-comedy *Frank Stubbs Promotes* with Timothy Spall. It wasn't long before she was filming the second series, but in between she managed to fit in the film *Mammy*, directed by Eurythmic Dave Stewart. Danniella also performed on the soundtrack to the film.

Ironically, one of Danniella's first jobs in showbusiness was as an Albert Square extra. An eleven-year-old Danniella once whizzed past Den and Angie on her roller skates!

ANNA WING (LOU BEALE) 1985–1988

So determined was Anna to get the part of Lou, that she went to the audition clutching the birth certificate that proved she was a genuine East Ender!

Born Eva Wing, she was an artist's model before she

became an actress. She then worked at her craft for fifty years before becoming a household name in *EastEnders* at the age of 71!

She married at thirty and had a son, Mark, but divorced three years later. Anna also has a son, Jon, by the poet Philip O'Connor.

Anna rarely appears on TV these days, but can be seen shopping in London's West End where she owns a restaurant.

ADAM WOODYATT (IAN BEALE)
1985–PRESENT DAY

Ian had been one of the most difficult roles to cast, and it was only at the last minute that a butcher's apprentice from Wales (his parents had recently moved there from Chingford, Essex) was summoned to London to audition for a part that would change his life. But that's exactly what happened to Adam.

Adam is one of the jokers on set, and will often tease screen wife Michelle Collins when they have to do a kissing scene. He thoroughly enjoys doing panto and tries to tread the boards every Christmas.

He is also a keen sports fan (he supports Liverpool FC) and can often be found in front of the telly between takes catching up on the latest results. Adam is one of the few remaining original cast members.